PLAYING WORD GAMES

JOHN SMYTH

STANLEY PAUL
LONDON

First published in 1995

1 3 5 7 9 10 8 6 4 2

First published in the United Kingdom in 1995 by
Stanley Paul and Company Limited,
an imprint of Random House,
20 Vauxhall Bridge Road,
London SW1V 2SA

Random House Australia (Pty) Limited,
20 Alfred Street, Milsoms Point, Sydney,
New South Wales 2061, Australia

Random House New Zealand Limited
18 Poland Road, Glenfield,
Auckland 10, New Zealand

Random House South Africa (Pty) Limited,
PO Box 337, Bergvlei, South Africa

Random House UK Limited Reg. No. 954009

ISBN 0 09 180772 7

Edited by Paul Barnett
Design and make-up from disk by Roger Walker

Printed and bound in Great Britain
by Clays Ltd, St Ives plc

CONTENTS

AUTHOR'S FOREWORD

When did people first start playing word games? There's no real answer to the question, but it seems almost certain that oral word games must have predated the written word, and written ones probably predated printing. It is likely, then, that among the word games we play today are descendants, perhaps changed only in their details, of some of the earliest games humanity invented.

And word games still *are* played today – on an extraordinarily wide scale. Their popularity can be gauged by the huge number of word-puzzle magazines on sale, by the large and enthusiastic following that Scrabble® maintains in diverse countries (many of which hold national championships), by the prevalence of crosswords in our newspapers and magazines … At a less formal level, if you look around the waiting area at any airport or railway station you're likely to see parents and children playing written games like Hangman or guessing games like Twenty Questions.

Some earnest postgraduate student somewhere must have laboured over an abstruse treatise explaining – or trying to – why we should find word games so fascinating. That is not my purpose in this book. Nor have I attempted to examine the history of the different kinds of wordplay; readers interested in this subject should turn to Tony Augarde's highly entertaining and informative book *The Oxford Guide to Word Games* (1984). There exist specialist guides to commercially produced pastimes like Lexicon® (sadly little seen today) and Scrabble®, so I have avoided discussion of these games. Instead what I have aimed to do is provide a guide to over fifty of the best word games (plus countless variations), some widely popular and others little known. Assisted by a carefully selected team of dedicated and on occasion appropriately oiled researchers (my friends), I have tried out all of these games rigorously over a period of years to ensure that they are truly worthy to receive the much-coveted Smyth Quality Hallmark. Where variant rules exist, the team and I have tested them to find which lead to the best game; in particular, we have adjusted – and in a few cases invented – scoring systems to achieve what we determined scientifically to be the most enjoyable results. I have included an additional short section on puzzle-setting, codes and ciphers, so that you can have fun irritating your friends by sending them bafflingly incomprehensible cryptic messages.

I have thoroughly enjoyed researching and compiling this book. If you, the reader, derive even a fraction of that enjoyment from it, then I shall consider my efforts successful.

I can hear my editor beginning to rumble the traditional words: 'That's enough forward – Ed.' So, without further ado, arm yourself with your doughty pencil and paper, take up your trusted dictionary and thesaurus, and prepare yourself mentally for a good old-fashioned wallow in logophilia* . . .

Good luck!

John Smyth
October 1994

* 'Logophilia' is a word curiously absent from most dictionaries, although its use is not particularly uncommon. It means, obviously, the love (possibly obsessive) of words. The person doing the loving is a logophile.

MEMO FROM THE TERMINOLOGY DEPARTMENT

The word 'athlete' – which used to imply, if nothing else, a certain degree of sweatiness – seems to have changed its meaning in recent years. Nowadays we have synchronized-swimming athletes, body-building athletes, golf athletes, darts athletes, snooker athletes … this last seeming particularly inapt since, at least in my university days, snooker was the lazy student's alternative to falling asleep in lectures.

However, where snooker athletes go, logophiles should not fear to follow. Realizing that the word 'player' is not always *le mot juste*, and anxious to avoid such verbal contortions as 'players playing wordplay games', I hit upon the useful neologism 'lexicographical athlete'.

Elegant though that term is, as I'm sure you'll agree, it is unfortunately a little cumbersome: fine for the presentation ceremony at some future Olympic Games, perhaps, but not ideal for everyday use. The contraction 'LexicAth' seemed for a while fashionably portmanteau, but eventually – in this, the Age of Acronyms and Initial-Speak – I settled for the simple 'LA', and have used it throughout.

So, step forward, LAs of the world!

JS

A NOTE ON DICTIONARIES

Some of the games described in this book assume you have access to a reasonably comprehensive dictionary.

In general, dictionaries fall into two classes: prescriptive and descriptive. This is to say that some of them tell you how words *ought* to be used, and others tell you *how* they are used. Within the past couple of decades or so, the division between the two classes has become much more blurred, primarily because the compilers of previously prescription-oriented dictionaries have realized the limitations such an approach imposes on the usefulness of the final compilation, but also because the advent of computers has made the updating of dictionaries a far easier task – it is no longer impossible for dictionaries to include usages that have become current within only a year or so before publication.

This is not to say that compiling dictionaries will ever be an easy or quick task. The advantage of using a really huge dictionary – the obvious example is *The Oxford English Dictionary* – is of course that it contains a truly staggering number of words, along with examples of their use and etymological details concerning their origin and derivation. The disadvantage is that, by its very nature, such a compilation will always be significantly out of date (although more frequent updates are now becoming possible, thanks to CD–ROM technology). *The Shorter Oxford English Dictionary* is more frequently revised but, depending as it does upon the full compilation, likewise tends to be considerably out of date in terms of neologisms and new usages of previously existing words; it does, however, contain much interesting material on derivations, with examples of literary usages. (The *Concise* and *Pocket* versions are generally too small for the dedicated word-gamer, although occasional games actually work better with what would otherwise be regarded as an inadequate dictionary: even the *Collins Little Gem* can have its uses.)

A good balance is achieved by the *Chambers English Dictionary* (earlier editions were called *Chambers Twentieth-Century Dictionary*). Although a much smaller book than, say, the Shorter Oxford, it in fact contains more words and definitions, at the expense of etymological and exemplary material. It still suffers a little from the prescriptive approach to which it adhered until quite recently, but its more arcane reaches are the delight of crossword compilers (many of the most difficult cryptic crosswords recommend it by name), Scrabble® enthusiasts and advanced word-gamers in general. Recent editions cope reasonably adequately with neologisms and new usages, although the omissions can sometimes be startling. Much better in this respect are the *Collins Dictionary of the English Language* (although it has far fewer words defined) and, in the USA, the various editions of *Webster's*, *Random House* and *American Heritage*.

When buying a dictionary, make sure you know what you're buying. It has become increasingly common to find old editions of well-known dictionaries reprinted as if they were new compilations, and sold as 'bargains'. Always check the copyright date (usually on the back of the title page) before you buy.

The same advice goes for thesauri. *Roget's Thesaurus* is the longest established, and is available in numerous editions. One of the best is *Roget's International Thesaurus*. Although not in fact truly international (it is a US compilation) it has good coverage of both UK and US usages, and a valuable additional feature is that it includes many extensive lists of types of things: birds, dances, musical forms, and so on – there's even one headed 'Philosophies'!

One word 'game' that is always overlooked is the simple pastime of browsing through the dictionary: some of the words you can uncover will by turns amuse, baffle and fascinate you. With this in mind, various compilers have produced dictionaries restricted to bizarre words; a good example is *Mrs Byrne's Dictionary of Unusual, Obscure and Preposterous Words* (1974) by Josefa Heifetz Byrne, but there are several others. Another useful book in this context is the *Concise Scots Dictionary* (1985); aside from its other pleasures, it contains a few useful words (e.g., 'swither', 'outwith') that have no direct equivalent in standard English.

It can sometimes be useful, before embarking on a competitive word game, to ensure that all participants are agreed on which dictionary will be used as the ultimate arbiter if there proves to be any dispute.

PART 1
ORAL GAMES

Many of our most popular parlour games are based on the spoken word. Most oral word games fall into one of three main categories:

▶ **GUESSING GAMES** – which involve deductive skills as LAs use question and answer to find a solution, and some of which may also be performance games

▶ **ROUND-THE-TABLE PING–PONG GAMES** – which rattle along from one LA to the next, speed of reaction and immediate vocabulary usually being the keys to success

▶ **MEMORY GAMES** – in which LAs rely on their ability to remember words (often a sequence of words) accurately and quickly

But let's start with a few games that fall into none of these categories . . .

There are various different versions of this game, but the basic principle is that you must, without undue hesitation, answer questions put to you without using certain words (or letters) that have beforehand been designated 'taboo'. Should you accidentally employ one of these words, your turn is over and somebody else (either the successful interrogator or the next person in the circle) becomes the responder. Questioners are allowed to use every conceivable ruse to trick you into using the taboo words: they can try to catch you by surprise with impertinent personal enquiries, bombard you with rapid-fire questions, make funny faces as they speak to you, or use any of a host of other strategies to disrupt your concentration. Your answers needn't be truthful, but they must be direct and plausible responses (in other words, you can't just reply with some meaningless gobbledygook phrase).

All you have to do is avoid those words which are taboo . . .

Sounds easy, doesn't it? Well, it ain't. If you can answer more than half a dozen questions without succumbing, you can reckon you're doing pretty well. Each question successfully negotiated can count for one point, with the winner being the person with most points after a certain number of rounds.

The simplest and commonest form of Taboo – you can even see it on television game-shows – is

NI OUI NI NON

otherwise known as the Yes and No Game. In this version you must answer all the questions put to you without using the words 'yes' or 'no'. Variations of them – 'yeah', 'yup', 'naw', 'nope', etc. – are likewise disallowed. A typical interchange might go something like this:

▶ **Are you pleased to be here?**
I was until you started asking me questions.

▶ **Is your name Betty?**
My full name is Elizabeth, but I'm usually called Betty.

▶ **Are you twenty-five years old?**
That is my age.

▶ **Do you know there's a toffee stuck to the back of your skirt?**
No! **** it! I put it on clean this morning. Where's . . . ? Oh. You swine . . .

VARIATIONS

▶ Dodge the Words

You have to avoid one or several predetermined common words – the longer the list of words, the more difficult the game. For reference, the commonest words in spoken English are 'the', 'and', 'I', 'to', 'of', 'a', 'you', 'that', 'in', 'it' and 'is'.

▶ Guess the Taboo

Here only one word is selected as forbidden, but you aren't told in advance which word it is. Instead, you have to deduce which types of words to avoid from the way the questions are couched – because obviously your interrogators will be framing their questions in such a way that you're likely inadvertently to use the word they have chosen. If you finally guess which word that is, you take another turn using a fresh taboo word. If your guess is wrong, though, your turn is over.

▶ Lipogram Taboo

Rather than whole words being forbidden, you are not allowed to use any words containing a particular letter – E, I or T, for example. This is a very difficult version of the game: you have to think fast to make sure your replies are safe. Clearly it helps if you keep your answers short.

There's no scoring in this game, which was apparently played by some of the wittier intimates of President John F. Kennedy, and may have been devised by them. Certainly it's an excellent game for punsters.

One person picks at random an 'answer' – the more bizarre or obscure the better – and the others must try to think up a question which could lead to that answer. The 'winner' is the person who produces the funniest or most ingenious question – usually the one that makes the answer seem 'inevitable'.

Here are some examples of answers you might question:

▶ **Slug sauce.**
What do you cut slugs in half with?

▶ **Annapolis.**
Who's ahead of Billy Banana in the fruitshop queue?

▶ **Sequins.**
And just how successful was your pregnancy, Mrs Roach?

▶ **9W.**
Mr Wagner, do you spell your name with a 'V'?

This is a venerable game that can be played almost anywhere. It works best with three or more LAs. The first LA calls out a letter, the next a second letter, the third a third letter, and so on. The object of the exercise is never to add a letter such that the sequence forms a word of four letters or more ('me' and 'men' are fine, but 'mend' is taboo).

At the same time, any letter you add to the sequence must be capable, when taken with its predecessors, of forming the first part of a word. If the next LA in turn doubts you, you can be challenged to name a complete word beginning with the letters so far supplied. Of course, you could try bluffing – adding a letter without having any 'target' word in mind, so that the problem is passed on to the next LA – but then you'd be vulnerable to a challenge.

The game gets more difficult the longer the sequence continues, because all the other LAs are attempting to reduce the options left open to the people coming after them: if the sequence has got as far as ANTIDISESTABLISHMEN by the time it's your turn, you really don't have a lot of choice! Rounds end when LAs inadvertently finish a word or when a challenge is issued: if the challenge succeeds, the defaulting LA loses, but if it fails (i.e., the LA can cite a valid 'target' word) the challenger is the one to lose.

There are various methods of scoring. Everyone except the loser can be given one point, with the points being added up at the end of the session to find out who is the winner. Alternatively, all LAs can be issued a set number of 'lives' at the start, forfeiting one of these each time they lose a round, the winner being the last person left 'alive'. When larger groups are playing a simple knockout system can be used, with the loser of each round dropping out until two stalwarts are left for the final contest. If you have a fair amount of time for the game, try using either of these two latter systems and awarding the winner of each set a point. The overall winner of the session is the person who first amasses a fixed number of points (e.g., three).

A typical game of Ghost between Winston, Jane and Joe might go like this:

▶ Winston opens with the letter **M**.

▶ Jane follows with E, making the sequence **ME**. There are lots of words starting **ME**, so obviously there's no challenge.

▶ Joe adds A, to make **MEA**.

▶ Winston realizes he can't add D, L, N or T, because those letters would form **MEAD**, **MEAL**, **MEAN** and **MEAT**, respectively. He therefore adds **S**.

▶ Jane wonders about challenging Winston, but then realizes **MEAS** comes at the start of **MEASLES**, **MEASURE** and so on. She therefore adds **U**, knowing that she is thereby safe from challenge herself.

▶ Joe has seen what is coming, and adds **R**.

▶ Winston has a new problem: he cannot add **E**, because that would complete the word. After a moment's thought he adds **I**.

▶ Jane immediately adds N, so the sequence is now MEASURIN.

▶ Joe is stuck, and knows it. He hastily adds **E** and adopts a sickly look of starkly unconvincing supercool.

▶ Winston, no idiot he, refuses to believe there's a word starting **MEASURINE**, and challenges.

▶ Joe is unable to supply a word, and so loses the round. (Note that Joe loses even had the dictionary shown that such a word existed. The important point is that LAs must know their offering is valid.)

▶ Jane (the next LA in sequence after Winston, who started the first round) begins the next round with a new letter.

Superghost is an advanced version of Ghost in which LAs can add letters to either the beginning or the end of the sequence, with the rules otherwise being the same. A round might go like this:

- N
- NA
- NAT
- RNAT
- ERNAT
- ERNATI
- TERNATI
- TERNATIO
- NTERNATIO
- NTERNATION
- NTERNATIONA
- NTERNATIONAL

Here the next LA has some slight quandary, because adding an 'I' to the start of the sequence seems inescapable. But then inspiration strikes: the LA remembers there are words like INTERNATIONALISM and INTERNATIONALIST, and thus freely adds an 'I' to form

- NTERNATIONALI

And so the round continues . . .

This is another variant of Ghost, having the same rules but being played with words instead of letters, the object being to avoid completing a sentence of three words or more. No more than two adjectives or adverbs may be supplied in a row – the game obviously becomes rapidly tedious if the sequence runs: 'I would like to eat a large, juicy, tasty, green, hot, steaming, salted, seasoned, squishy . . .'

The advantage of this game over the other versions of Ghost is that it is easier to remember a string of words than a sequence of letters, so the game is better suited for playing in places where there might be a lot of distraction – on a bus, for example. However, the game isn't as simple as it seems, because LAs can challenge at any point, claiming a sentence has been completed. In fact, it can be extremely difficult not to finish a sentence inadvertently. To see why, think of this sentence: 'I would like to go along to the shop.' At first glance you might think that the LA who added the word 'shop' was the loser, but – assuming the LAs were alert – the game would have ended long before then, because the following are also valid sentences:

- I would like to.
- I would like to go.
- I would like to go along.

GUESSING GAMES

Guessing games are like detective stories: the LAs who are acting as detectives must use clues given to them by another LA or LAs – usually in response to questions – in order to solve the mystery. There are countless different guessing games: what follows is a selection of the best and most popular.

This is the classic oral guessing game. One LA thinks of an object, and will answer either 'yes' or 'no' to questions asked about it. Traditionally, one 'free' piece of information is supplied to the other LAs before the questioning starts: the LA announces that the object falls into one or more of the following categories

▶ **ANIMAL** (including people and also animal products like butter, leather, wool, fishpaste and gossamer)
▶ **VEGETABLE** (including vegetable products like paper, linen, rubber, tofu and olive oil)
▶ **MINERAL** (including anything that is not and never has been alive, like steam, brickwork, whitewash and the sun)
▶ **ABSTRACT** (including anything non-material, like the sky, a reflection in the mirror, lechery and the spectrum)

Obviously there can be occasional difficulties with this classification scheme; for example, coal could be thought of as either vegetable or mineral. Here the LA who has thought of the object must use judgement to give as fair an assessment as possible: coal might be described as 'mineral with vegetable connotations' or even just as 'mineral and vegetable'.

The other LAs are allowed up to 20 questions, including direct guesses, to establish what the object could be. If after those 20 questions have been asked the answer has still not emerged, the LA who thought of the object is the winner and receives one point, and starts over again by thinking of another object. If someone makes a wrong guess during the questioning, they must drop out of the round. But, if someone makes a correct guess before the 20 questions are up, the round is over and they receive one point and must think of an object to start the next round. The person with the most points at the end of the session is the winner.

CONTINUED... ▶

A mere 20 questions doesn't seem like very many, especially when the answers are so restricted, but in fact you can expect the questioners to be successful more often than not.

Jane has thought of a pack of Tarot cards as her object, and the other LAs have 20 questions in which to establish this. The start of the round might go like this:

▶ **Jane:** 'My object is mainly vegetable, but likely has some mineral and possibly some animal in it as well.' (She is thinking of the inks, the glue in the card, and so on.)

▶ **Question:** 'Is it alive?'

▶ **Jane:** 'No.'

▶ **Question:** 'Would you or anyone else wear it?'

▶ **Jane:** 'No.'

▶ **Question:** 'Can you eat it?'

▶ **Jane:** 'No.'

▶ **Question:** 'Would you show it to your friends among mixed company?'

▶ **Jane:** 'Yes.'

And so on. Sometimes people play the game without answers being restricted to 'yes' or 'no'. 'It depends', 'sort of' and 'occasionally' among other responses may be used in some circles.

This has rules very similar to those of Twenty Questions, the major exceptions being

▶ LAs are not disqualified for making wrong guesses – indeed, those guesses may be regarded as partial solutions

▶ there is no limit to the number of questions that may be asked.

Equally, though, there is no limit on the obscurity of the thing (if thing it is) that the starting LA may choose as the mystery item. Here are some possibilities:

▶ the vision of democracy in the minds of the signatories to the First Amendment

▶ Sir Peter Lely making a swift estimate of the number of warts on Oliver Cromwell's face before starting work on the Protector's portrait

▶ the reflection of moonlight on Lake Lucerne in September

▶ Napoleon slipping on a patch of ice during the retreat from Moscow

Obviously this is a much longer game than Twenty Questions! However, as with Twenty Questions, the task of the questioners is not nearly as difficult as it might appear: an hour or three is usually more than long enough for a sufficiently precise guess to emerge – 'sufficiently precise' because, for example, it wouldn't be necessary for the questioners to identify by name the portraitist, Lely, to whom Cromwell addressed his famous 'warts and all' remark.

Precisely because it is a long game, Infinity Questions is usually played just for fun rather than for scores. However, dedicated enthusiasts can adopt the Twenty Questions scoring system, keeping a tally over a period of weeks or months.

I n Botticelli one LA (let's say it's Jill) thinks of a person – either famous or at least known to everyone in the group (fictional characters are allowable) – and 'becomes' that person. The other LAs must try to find out who Jill has 'become' using a somewhat more elaborate questioning system than that employed in Twenty Questions.

Each of the interrogators in turn must first ask a general-knowledge question. If Jill knows the answer to this, the LA's turn is over. If, however, Jill doesn't know the answer, the LA is then allowed to ask a question directly pertaining to the mystery person. These direct questions must be of the form that expects a 'yes' or 'no' answer, or must be couched in either/or form. Specific questions like 'What is your first name?' are disallowed. After (or, indeed, before) this second question, the LA may make a guess as to who Jill has 'become'. If this guess is right, the LA is the winner of the round. If it's wrong, the LA must drop out. If no one guesses Jill's adopted identity within a certain time, or if everybody gives up, then she is the round's winner.

There is one important extra rule. LAs must themselves know the correct answers to the general-knowledge questions they ask. If they do not, they either forfeit their turn or – local rules differ – must drop out of the round.

Instead of general knowledge, the LAs' first questions can be limited to a particular field of the group's (or Jill's) choosing: cinema, geography, politics, rock music, television . . .

A typical set of exchanges in a game of Botticelli would be:

▶ **Tom:** 'What is the capital of Paraguay?'

▶ **Jill:** 'I don't know.'

▶ **Tom:** 'It's Asunción. Are you a rock star?'

▶ **Jill:** 'Yes.'

▶ **Tom:** 'Are you David Bowie?'

▶ **Jill:** 'No.'

▶ **Robert:** 'What colour is at the other end of the spectrum from red?'

▶ **Jill:** 'Um . . . blue?'

▶ **Robert:** 'No. Indigo. Are you . . . ?'

▶ **Everybody:** 'Robert gave the wrong answer. It should be violet. It's Alice's turn . . .'

And so on.

This is another game of the Twenty Questions variety. As in Botticelli, LAs must try to identify a real or fictional character by using questions of a particular type.

A very particular type, in this instance! Let's say the person who has chosen to 'become' the mystery character is Peter. The other LAs must ask Peter to come up with particular metaphors or similes that would apply to his choice. Their questions thus take the form 'And if you were a drink, you would be . . . ?', 'And if you were an animal, you would be . . . ?', and so on.

Imagine Peter has decided to 'become' Obelix, the strong, plump, genial and somewhat simple-minded chum of Asterix the Gaul. The first questioner asks: 'And if you were a country, you would be . . . ?' Now Peter has a wide variety of possible answers. For example:

▶ **Germany** – a large country whose people, by the standards of other European nations, eat heavy food and in large quantities
▶ **Argentina** – the colours of whose flag match those of Obelix's outfit
▶ **Australia** – an extremely large country, much of which is vacant
▶ **the United States** – another extremely large country, and of course a very strong one

Whatever Peter answers will in itself not give much of a clue, because there are dozens of other countries he might have chosen for different reasons. However, the sum total of his answers after several rounds of questioning should narrow things down sufficiently for sensible guessing to start.

In this guessing game the mystery item is a verb. One of the LAs thinks of a verb and the others try to discover it by asking him or her questions in which the unknown verb is substituted by the words 'coffee pot'. Typical questions might therefore be:

▶ Do you often coffee pot in the kitchen?
▶ How many times a week do you coffee pot?
▶ Have you coffee potted at all today?
▶ Do you ever coffee pot at the office?

Clearly this game can very rapidly become indecorous . . . which, depending on the company, may be a large part of its appeal. You can either just play it for fun or establish a scoring system like that for Twenty Questions, with the total number of questions limited to 20 all told, or five per LA.

This is one of the classic word games: almost everybody must have played it as a child and/or, in adulthood, played it with children. There are two slightly different versions of the game, but both start with the LA whose turn it is looking around to find an object that everyone can see – the table, for example – and saying, 'I spy with my little eye something beginning with T.'

In the simpler version, the one most often played with children and ideal for use on long car journeys, everyone takes turns guessing what the object could be (teapot, tapestry, transom, etc.) until either someone gets the right answer – in which case it is their turn to choose an object – or everyone gives up, in which case the original LA selects another object.

Adults may prefer the second version, in which LAs may ask a number of yes/no questions about the object, such as

▶ Is it green?
▶ Is it bigger than me?
▶ Could I eat it?

Generally, questions relating to the location of the object rather than its nature ('Is it hanging on the wall?') are disallowed.

The exact number of questions each LA is permitted depends on the number of LAs: the fewer the questioners, the more questions each should be allowed. As a rule of thumb, the total number should be not more than 10 – otherwise the game becomes too easy.

This is an excellent guessing game which can be played at different levels of difficulty by people of all ages.

One of the LAs – let's assume it's Adam – thinks of a word and gives the others a clue to it in the form: 'I have a word that rhymes with . . .'. For example, if Adam's chosen word were 'brad', he might say: 'I have a word that rhymes with "had".' The other LAs – the Rhyming Toms – must ask questions that allude to words which likewise rhyme with 'had', and Adam must guess the word they're referring to and tell them whether they are right or wrong. The game might proceed like this:

▶ **Adam:** 'I have a word that rhymes with "had".'

▶ **Jackie:** 'Is it a young Scot?'

▶ **Adam:** 'No, Rhyming Tom, it isn't a "lad".'

Jackie's turn is now over, and the questioning passes to the next person, Mike:

▶ **Mike:** 'Is it something very small?'

▶ **Adam:** 'No, Rhyming Tom, it isn't . . . um . . .'

▶ **Mike:** 'The word I was after is "tad".'

Because Adam failed to guess Mike's word, Mike is now free to ask another question in the same form. This might be:

▶ **Mike:** 'Is it a smallish nail?'

▶ **Adam:** 'Yes, Rhyming Tom, it's a "brad".'

Mike has thus won the round, and will take over the central role for the next one. Clearly, if no one had been able to guess the word 'brad', Adam would have been the winner and would have set the problem for the next round. Depending on the number of people in the company, the interrogators can either drop out of the round whenever they ask an unsuccessful question or can be given at the start a certain number of 'lives', losing one each time their question fails until there are no more Rhyming Toms left 'alive' or someone has made a successful guess.

This game can cause arguments and accusations of cheating, so Adam would be wise to write down his selected word on a sheet of paper before the questioning begins.

This is a very simple game in principle but can lead to a lot of fun. One of the LAs chooses something in the traditional way – it can be an object, a person or a place, and can be real or fictional – and then, without revealing what the item is, offers the other LAs a description of it. Each LA in turn is then allowed to ask a question demanding the answer 'yes' or 'no' until someone guesses the correct answer. LAs who guess wrongly are knocked out of the round. If no one comes up with the right answer the winner is the LA who set the puzzle.

The great skill of Descriptions lies, obviously, in the description itself: this cannot be outright false, but you can be significantly economical with the truth! You can supply only a partial description, on the basis of which the other LAs are likely to make completely erroneous guesses. Or you could bamboozle them by playing up some of the mystery item's lesser-known characteristics as if they were major ones. Pretend you're a Government spokesman telling the full and honest truth and you won't go far wrong.

This is a quick-fire game that offers tremendous entertainment – and also often demands a fair amount of mental effort, especially on the part of the problem-setter.

One of the LAs, Matt, thinks of a famous person – either real or fictional – and offers the rest of the group a clue in the form of a descriptive phrase based on the mystery person's initials. If for example Matt has chosen Abraham Lincoln, the clue he announces to the other LAs might be one of

▶ American leader
▶ able lawyer
▶ assassinated legislator
▶ avowed liberator

If no one can guess who is being referred to, Matt must offer a further clue in the same form, and so on until finally someone guesses the right answer. This is why the game can be so difficult for the problem-setter! If the other LAs are having an off-day, Matt may soon run out of ideas for appropriate phrases . . .

This is a sort of stripped-down version of Descriptions: it tends to be faster-moving and is easier to play in places where there are likely to be distractions – cafés, for example. In this game the description of the selected item is limited to merely five descriptive keywords (which may be words or simple phrases). If the problem-setter, Jennifer, has decided on Humphrey Bogart as the mystery item, the keywords she announces to the company might be:

▶ movies
▶ USA
▶ lisp
▶ Oscar
▶ thrillers

Unlike the case in Descriptions, the other LAs are not allowed to ask Jennifer any questions – the five keywords should be enough.

VARIATIONS

▶ The Adjective Game

As in the straightforward version, Jennifer must give five keywords, but these are restricted to descriptive adjectives. If she has chosen coffee as her mystery object, a valid set of adjectives would be

▶ liquid
▶ black
▶ strong
▶ delicious
▶ addictive

▶ The VAN Game

In this variant Jennifer gives the other LAs only three words as clues: a verb, an adjective and a noun (hence VAN). Her VAN keywords might be:

▶ (sip) verb
▶ (black) adjective
▶ (stimulant) noun

Because the information offered is so limited, LAs of the VAN Game are each allowed to ask Jennifer a yes/no question, as in Descriptions.

This fast-moving game differs from most other guessing games in that there is no single LA who is the problem-setter. Instead, all the LAs are involved in both setting and solving clues.

Any LA – Katrina, for example – picks a four-letter word (or a five-letter word, for more advanced LAs) to start the game. She might open a book at random and let her eye run down the page until she sees one, or she could simply pluck a word out of her head. Either way, she tells the group what word she has chosen. Next Katrina must think of another word that can be made by altering only one of the letters in the start-word, and she offers a clue to this word to another LA. That LA must try to solve the clue, then form a new word the same way and offer a clue to the next LA … and so on round the group. If the word Katrina has chosen is 'role', the round could start like this:

▶ **Katrina:** 'Kapil, the clue to my new word is: you can use it to climb with.'

▶ **Kapil:** 'You can use **rope** to climb with. Don, apples like this are nice and sweet.'

▶ **Don:** 'Apples are nice and sweet when they're **ripe**. Lois, little birds do this.'

▶ **Lois:** 'Little birds shriek for food, whistle, sing, fall out of the air when Don goes by . . . oh, yes, they **pipe**. Roger, if you were a heartsick lover you might do this …'

LAs can be given a number of 'lives' at the start, forfeiting one of them every time they are knocked out of the round through either failing to solve one of the clues or being unable to think of a new word that can be formed from the previous one. The winner is the person still 'alive' after everyone else has dropped out.

NOTE:

For a more difficult version of Clue Word Chains, only the first word is given out loud. Each LA in turn solves the clue offered to them without announcing the solution, forms a new word, and then passes on a new clue. LAs unable either to solve a clue or to construct a new word according to the rules can try to bluff things out – hoping that the next person in line will both have deduced the previous word and be able to form a new word on the basis of an appropriately bland clue.

For example, imagine you had been able to follow developments as far as the LA ahead of you, June, who was given a clue that led to the word 'tooth'. She offers you the clue that her new word is something you might plight. Unable (perhaps because distracted) to guess that her word is 'troth', you nevertheless look intelligent and offer the next LA the clue that this is something connected with the morning. This is actually a very vague clue, but with luck your neighbour will assume you mean 'froth', as when brushing your teeth, or 'broth', which you might eat at breakfast, or . . .

Your neighbour may of course be not so silly, and challenge you. If you can't think of a word that would fit the bill (remember, you still don't know what word it was the previous LA gave you), then you are knocked out of the round and lose a life. Any unsuccessful challenge means, of course, that the challenger suffers this same fate.

Quiz Queues is really a party game, requiring at least 15 people if it is to work at its best. Because it is a race, it can get pretty boisterous. It can be used early on as an ice-breaker or, later, for a bit of knockabout fun.

You need an odd number of LAs. These line up to form two equal queues. The LA left over – Jim in this case – is the Quizmaster for the round. He stands facing the two queues and addresses to the two LAs at the backs of the queues a quiz question – about general knowledge, trivia, sport, the movies or whatever subject has been agreed beforehand. (If neither of the LAs at the rear know the answer, Jim must ask them another question. If both fail to answer five times in a row, the LAs at the fronts of the queues go to the back and the round starts again.)

The two LAs at the rear must whisper their answers to the LAs directly in front of them, taking care to keep their voices low enough that no one else can hear. The pair who have just received the message must in turn pass it on in a whisper to the next LAs ahead of them in the queue, and so on until the answer reaches the LAs right at the front, who shout it at Jim.

The first queue to deliver the correct answer to Jim in this way is the winner. The person at its front becomes the new Quizmaster, while Jim himself goes to the back of that queue, ready for the start of the next round.

NOTE:

Quiz Queues, like many other word games, depends for its success on all the LAs being honest. The only LAs allowed to offer answers to the questions are the pair at the rear. Other LAs must relay as faithfully as they can the answers whispered to them: even if they know an answer is wrong, they can't change it.

Of course sometimes, because of the Chinese Whispers effect (see page 38), the LA at the rear may have supplied the right answer, only to hear a completely wrong one delivered from the front of the queue!

This is both a word game and a performance game: it requires LAs to use both guesswork and miming. It can get pretty physical, so it's a good idea to make sure there's plenty of space and that nothing could get knocked over or broken.

One LA, Elizabeth, thinks of an adverb. The other LAs take turns in asking her to perform actions 'in the manner of the word' – that is, according to the adverb she has chosen. Imagine she has selected the adverb 'clumsily' (I did mention this game could get reasonably physical). Other LAs may instruct her to

▶ **drink in the manner of the word**

(Elizabeth spills her drink all over the front of her dress)

▶ **speak in the manner of the word**

(Elizabeth mumbles some spittle-spraying gobbledygook)

▶ **jump in the manner of the word**

(Elizabeth falls over as she lands)

▶ **eat in the manner of the word**

(look, you don't really want a description of what Elizabeth does here, do you?)

The person who guesses the mystery adverb is the winner of the round, and takes over from Elizabeth, choosing another word to do things 'in the manner of'.

NOTE:

A really creepy variant of Adverbs is where one LA – Elizabeth again – goes out of the room and all the rest decide among themselves what the mystery adverb shall be. When she is allowed back in, she asks her erstwhile friends to perform actions 'in the manner of the word', as before. Meanwhile, everything else that the others in the group are doing incidentally – taking a gulp of their drink, shifting in their seat, and so on – is likewise done according to the chosen adverb.

The combined effect of such a performance can be quite overpowering in a manner that is hard to describe: certainly the solitary person should not be a child, who might get very upset. To get an idea of why I've described this variant as 'creepy', assume that the adverb selected is 'grovellingly'. Now imagine *a whole roomful* of people acting grovellingly towards you . . .

A classic parlour game, a classic word game, a classic guessing game, a classic performance game – there can hardly be any doubt that Charades is, well, a classic!

The puzzle can be posed by a single person and solved by the rest of the company, but in the most popular version of the game the company splits up into two teams. Each team takes turns in miming the parts (syllables, words or groups of words) of a well-known phrase, book title, movie title or famous person's name, concluding with a mime intended to represent the phrase/title/name as a whole. It is the task of the other team to guess the answer. You can really go to town in this version of the game, emulating the characters in Victorian novels and Golden Age detective stories by planning the production well in advance and going in for fancy dress and even make-up.

In another very popular version (it was made the basis of a television game some years ago) the company again divides into two teams. This time, however, when one team has chosen the phrase/name/title they tell a single member of the opposing team (Alice, say) what they have decided, and it is up to her to use mime to try to convey the subject to the rest of her team. Alice is permitted a little direct communication with the rest of her team, according to well established conventions: see opposite. Generally a time limit – perhaps two or three minutes – is set on their efforts.

Both versions allow plenty of scope for would-be actors, and also for punsters: the mime is to convey the *sound* of the various words or syllables rather than their spelling. For example, the title of Charles Dickens's *A Tale of Two Cities* might be broken down as

▶ a
▶ tail
▶ off
▶ to (perhaps indicated by pointing a finger)
▶ sit
▶ ease

The longer and more involved the phrase/name/title, and the more tortuous and far-fetched the breakdown, the better the fun usually is. However, especially when the company includes people who have never played the game before, it's a good idea to warm up with a few easy subjects.

COMMON GESTURES

▶ **Holding up a number of fingers**

Done at the start, this tells the other LAs how many words there are in the target phrase/name/title. Later on, the number of fingers you hold up indicates which word you're about to mime (one finger for the first word, two for the second, and so on), and likewise the position (number) of the syllable within that word.

▶ **Pretending you're operating an old-fashioned hand-wound movie camera**

It's a movie title.

▶ **Pretending you're reading**

It's a book title.

▶ **A hand cupped to the ear**

This means that the word or syllable you're about to mime rhymes with the relevant part of the phrase/name/title. If the title were *Gone With the Wind*, for the first word you might *yawn*, or look sickly and *wan*, or cheat by pointing at an LA called *Ron*.

▶ **Half-clenching the fingers and thumb, leaving a small gap in the clench**

This indicates a short word, usually a preposition or other function word, or possible a prefix: 'a', 'an', 'at', 'ex-', 'in' …

▶ **Crossing two hands or fingers to form a 'T'**

This indicates the word 'the'.

▶ **A vigorous shake of the head, or an upraised palm**

Someone has guessed wrongly, or is pursuing entirely the wrong line of reasoning. (Other appropriately graphic gesticulations may be deployed.)

▶ **A thumbs-up sign**

Someone has just guessed a syllable or word correctly.

hese aren't strictly word games, but they're close enough cousins that it'd be a definite lacuna if I missed them out. The setter describes a bizarre, apparently absurd situation and the other LAs must guess the explanation for it, generally through asking questions to elicit further information. To get the hang of Enigmas, take a look at the four below, which can be 'solved' without any extra details. Do try to puzzle them out before you look at the solutions!

▶ Enigma 1

A man goes into a bar and asks for a drink of water. The barman takes a gun from under the counter and points it at the man's head. The man says 'Thank you!' and walks out. Why?

▶ Enigma 2

Found lying in the middle of a field are a hat, a pipe, a scarf, a carrot and a couple of lumps of coal. Why?

▶ Enigma 3

A man lives on the 20th floor of an apartment block. He takes the elevator down to the ground floor on his way to work each morning, but when he comes home he rides up only as far as the 12th floor, then walks the rest of the way. Why?

▶ Enigma 4

Shades of the *Mary Celeste*! An empty ship is drifting in calm waters, far from any harbour, and is in no danger of sinking. There aren't any signs of fighting and, although no one has left the ship, there are no emergency liferafts or lifebelts. No other ship was responsible for leaving this one here, and it hasn't been reported missing. Why?

SOLUTIONS

▶ **Solution 1**   The man wanted water because he had hiccups. Noticing this, the barman chose instead to give him a fright. This banished the hiccups, so the man no longer needed the water.

▶ **Solution 2**   A snowman has melted with the thaw.

▶ **Solution 3**   The man is a midget and can reach up only as far as the 12th button in the elevator.

▶ **Solution 4**   It's a plastic toy ship afloat in a bathtub!

To play the game with friends, it's better to use Enigmas that are not self-contained, like the previous four, but require further elaboration (obtained through question-and-answer) before they can be fully 'solved'. After a bit of practice you should be able to invent appropriately weird situations yourself, but here are some to get you started:

▶ Enigma 5

A man driving along the road hears something, and promptly shoots himself. Why?

▶ Enigma 6

A dead man is found lying naked in a snow-covered field, with no footprints visible anywhere around him. Why?

▶ Enigma 7

A murderer is caught red-handed. In court, the prosecution seeks the death sentence, but the judge feels obliged to let the killer go. Why?

▶ Enigma 8

Billy, in a state of worry and bewilderment, is sitting on the floor on the middle of the room, even though the room also contains a chair, a bed, bedside table and another table. Why?

▶ Enigma 9

This is a locked-room mystery. There is nobody in the house and no one has broken in, but a couple are lying dead on the bedroom floor. All the doors and windows in the house are locked and intact, although there is broken glass on the floor, at which a chihuahua is barking. This wasn't a double suicide: the couple were definitely killed – as Sherlock Holmes realized immediately. Why?

CONTINUED... ▶

SOLUTIONS

▶ Solution 5

The man is a radio disc jockey, and has just murdered his wife. As alibi, he pre-recorded this morning's show. Listening on the car radio, he has just heard a fault on the tape he made. Realizing his alibi is now blown, he kills himself rather than face justice.

▶ Solution 6

The man was one of a party travelling by balloon. Because of a leak, the balloon was descending rapidly. In traditional fashion, the passengers threw out every excess bit of weight they could, including their own clothes. Still this wasn't enough. Nobody liked Bloggins much anyway, so . . .

▶ Solution 7

The murderer was a Siamese twin; his other half was present when the crime was committed but took no part in it – and in fact is the person who 'shopped' the killer. The judge refuses to let an innocent man be punished.

▶ Solution 8

Billy is a circus dwarf. As an April Fool joke his colleagues have sawn off the legs of all the furniture in his caravan. Billy has come into his caravan and thinks he must suddenly have grown taller, so that he will lose his job at the circus.

▶ Solution 9

The couple are a pair of goldfish. They died because the chihuahua knocked over their bowl.

Of course, it is possible that LAs may come up with 'better' solutions to Enigmas 5–9 than the ones given here, and this is true in general of this class of Enigma. If this happens, acknowledge their inventiveness with a good grace – but explain that the game is all about deducing the solution that *you* decided on!

ROUND-THE-TABLE PING-PONG GAMES

Of course, they needn't be done just round the table! These fast-action games can be played anywhere: on trains and buses, in bed – even over the telephone. They can be played by just two LAs, although usually they're designed for three or more.

Let's start off with an easy one so you can get the hang of things.

The object here is speed: anyone who can't respond within five seconds (or 10 seconds if playing with children, etc.) is out of the round – as is anyone whose offering is generally felt to be in violation of the rules.

The first LA calls out a noun or verb, selected at random – you could open a book and choose the first word on the page. The next LA must respond with a word whose meaning is connected with it in some way. The third LA must do likewise for this new word, and so on round and round the group. As the group gets smaller you can reduce the amount of reaction-time allowed to the LAs.

A typical sequence might be:

> tennis
> elbow
> bend
> river
> flow
> chart
> map
> locate
> uncover
> strip
> paint

Aside from the straightforward fun of playing Associations, what's particularly interesting about the game is the flow of meanings: after only a very few turns, the words generally have not the remotest connection with the one that started the round.

This is a very old game, and has been played not only in the parlour but also between lovers. You often find versions of its central ditty in handwritten Valentine's Day cards sent during the Victorian era.

The first LA, Melissa, has the letter A, and must find an appropriate adjective, person's name and place-name starting with that letter. She gives these in the form

▶ I love my love because he is **adorable**.
▶ His name is **Alphonse**.
▶ He lives in **Amsterdam**.

The next LA, Mosim, takes up the theme using the letter B:

▶ I love my love because she is **bounteous**.
▶ Her name is **Buffy**.
▶ She lives in **Boston**.

After Mosim has said this, the next LA must use the letter C:

▶ I love my love because she is **caring**.
▶ Her name is **Cindy**.
▶ She lives in **Cambridge**.

The next LA must use D, and so on until the alphabet has been used up (you may decide to leave out difficult letters like X), at which point you start all over again at A. Of course, no word or name may be re-used. LAs drop out if they are unable to think of three appropriate names/adjectives within a set period of time (e.g., 10 seconds).

This game is very similar to I Love My Love. The LA is asked two questions – 'Where are you going?' and 'What will you do there?' – and must respond using words that start with the appropriate letter of the alphabet. The first LA must name a place beginning with the letter A; the response to the second question must be in the form of a verb, adjective and noun, all three beginning with A. Here's a typical start:

▶ **Where are you going?**
Arkansas.

▶ **What will you do there?**
Arrest antisocial arsonists.

▶ **Where are you going?**
Birmingham.

▶ **What will you do there?**
Buy brass bedsteads.

▶ **Where are you going?**
California.

▶ **What will you do there?**
Collect cooperative concubines.

The game continues on through the alphabet – as with I Love My Love, you may decide beforehand to skip letters like X – and, on reaching the end, starts again at A, with no repetition of names or words being permitted.

This game is more difficult than I Love My Love – it can be tricky thinking of a convincing verb/adjective/noun triplet – so LAs should be allowed a longer period of thinking-time before being adjudged at fault and having to drop out of the round. LAs may also be disqualified if their verb/adjective/noun sentence is generally regarded as nonsensical – Arrest adoptive apples, for example.

Everyone together decides on a theme – even better, they could ask someone who isn't going to be playing the game to choose one for them. Using this theme, they must work through the alphabet calling out appropriate words beginning with each successive letter.

The themes can be as diverse or as limiting as the LAs want –

▶ kings and queens

▶ fruits

▶ women writers

▶ the television programmes I really hate

would all be suitable topics. As in earlier alphabetical games, after the alphabet has been gone round once you can start over again with A, B, . . . The LAs can decide beforehand to skip difficult letters like X and Q (particularly if the theme involves names of any kind). Each LA should be given a reasonable time to come up with a response; I can't recommend a precise time since the difficulty of this game depends so much on the particular topic chosen. Defaulting LAs drop out until only one is left.

A typical round, the theme chosen being women writers, could start like this:

▶ Jane **A**usten

▶ Charlotte **B**rontë

▶ Agatha **C**hristie

▶ Margaret **D**rabble

▶ George **E**liot

▶ Antonia **F**raser

▶ Elizabeth **G**askell

▶ Susan **H**ill

▶ P. D. **J**ames …

VARIATIONS

▶ Letter Themes

The rules are identical with the main game of Alphabetical Themes except that, instead of each LA finding a name or word starting with the next letter of the alphabet, in every round all LAs must find an appropriate name or word starting with the same letter. At the end of the round, the LAs move on one letter in the alphabet. Thus four LAs with fruit as their theme might start:

▶ apple
▶ apricot
▶ alligator pear
▶ avocado (yes – it is a fruit!)
▶ blueberry
▶ blackberry
▶ bilberry
▶ boysenberry
▶ cherry
▶ citron ...

Alternatively, a starting letter can be determined at random – e.g., by opening a book at any page and using the first letter on that page. Play continues until one person cannot think of an example, at which point they drop out and the

This is rather like Alphabetical Themes. However, instead of each new word starting with the next letter of the alphabet, it must start with the last letter of the preceding word. The first theme-word can be selected at random by one of the LAs, or a non-LA may be asked to supply one. No repetitions are permitted. A typical round, with the theme of animals, might thus start:

▶ dog
▶ goat
▶ tiger
▶ rat
▶ tapir
▶ roc
▶ chihuahua
▶ ass ...

Other rules are as for Alphabetical Themes.

This is an easier theme game, particularly enjoyed by younger children, because you are not restricted by the alphabet. A topic is selected and LAs must each, in turn, call out a word or name which can be associated with that topic. Before you start the game, you need to establish the order of LAs so that everyone knows whose turn is next. The game is more exciting if there is a time limit of 5–10 seconds or so for each player to think of a word – in which case you need a timekeeper who can also judge whether the words chosen are valid. Of course, LAs must be prepared to defend their words if challenged. The round ends when an LA cannot come up with an appropriate word, and a new theme is chosen.

You will find that if you choose a broad topic (something like music, sport or food) rounds can go on for ages. So it is best to think of more limited themes – like Batman, goldfish or the Eiffel Tower – unless very young children are playing (they will obviously have smaller vocabularies and a more limited general knowledge than older children and adults).

If you want to score this game, you can either allot each LA a set number of 'lives' at the outset, with one 'life' being forfeit whenever an LA loses a round, or you can operate a simple knockout system, with LAs dropping out every time they lose a round. Either way, the game continues until only the winner is left.

This is another theme game. It starts off easy but soon becomes much more difficult.

The theme is numbers, and the aim is for the LAs in turn to come up with words, phrases or titles associated with them. The game starts with one, typical examples of valid contributions being

▶ one-horse town
▶ one-man dog
▶ the first Noël
▶ *It Happened One Night*
▶ one-step
▶ 'Oneder' Woman

This last entry would almost certainly lead to immediate disqualification of the LA concerned – although local rules differ (in some circles it might be regarded as an excellent offering!) – and hence the end of the round. Otherwise rounds end when an LA can't think of a new example.

In the next round the association must be with the number two, in the next with the number three, and so on. You'll find that higher numbers present much more difficulty, especially those over 10: you might decide simply to have a catch-all 'over 10' round as the game's conclusion.

Local rules may allow the use of synonyms for the numbers: ace, singleton, brace, pair, trio, triplet, dozen, score and so on. For obvious reasons it's wise to outlaw from the start such putative entries as 'one o'clock' and 'the 1st of November'.

This is the simplest of several good rhyming games. A word of advice first:

You may find that you and your friends start playing them in the middle of conversations or when you should be talking about something else, and this can infuriate your other, non-rhymester friends.

In Rhyme Ping–Pong the first LA chooses a one-syllable word at random – perhaps by finding it in a book or newspaper – and calls it out. Each LA in turn must then supply a rhyming word (no repetitions allowed), the turn going around the group repeatedly until someone gets stuck. At that point a new word is chosen and a fresh round begins. If the word 'dog' were chosen as the starting point, the next few turns might run

▶ cog
▶ flog
▶ groundhog
▶ sprog . . .

Most often the game is played non-competitively, more as a pastime than anything else. However, if you want to score it you could use either a straightforward knockout system or allot LAs a set number of 'lives', with one of these being lost every time an LA defaults. Either way, the game continues until only the winner is left.

This is a game best played in a group of five or more. The first LA starts by announcing the opening line of a putative poem:

▶ If you go out in the woods today

The next LA has to produce the succeeding line of the poem, which must rhyme with the first, and then start a new rhyming pair with the poem's third line:

▶ You'll see teddy-bears making hay,
   Just the way they always do

The third LA has to make the second half of this new rhyming couplet, then start another:

▶ When they are expecting you.
   Sometimes they stop to eat an orange

. . . which is where the fun begins (well, you find a rhyme for 'orange'!). Rhymes may be as excruciating as the LAs' stomachs allow, with special accolades being awarded for fiendish ingenuity and general mental pervertedness.

The game is normally played non-competitively – in which case there is a further rule. Since the art of the game is to give the next LA the most impossible word with which to try to make a rhyme, the chances are that he or she will be stuck. In that event, the LA who produced the offending word must complete the rhyming couplet and then start a fresh one, with the order of play now going in the opposite direction from before.

This is quite a difficult game – and it's non-competitive – but if you're lucky the results can more than recompense you for your mental labours. Unlike most other rhyming games, it is best done with only two or three LAs, the precise rules varying depending on the exact number.

The aim is, of course, to compose a limerick. Assuming two LAs, Bill and Ben, the rhyming lines are contributed according to the following scheme:

▶ **Bill:** The picture of Dorian Gray

▶ **Ben**: Was carefully hidden away.
While he wenched and toss-potted

▶ **Bill**: The painted face rotted,
Leaving Dorian Gray quite OK.*

It is then Ben's turn to start the next limerick. If Buffy had joined the game, she rather than Bill would have been expected to contribute the final couplet, and it would have been she who started the new limerick.

It is quite a good idea to have a non-participating LA decide upon a topic for the limerick. And it is important that everyone enters into the challenge with good humour and that LAs allow the rules to be swayed occasionally. For instance, if the subject chosen was *Lady Chatterley's Lover*, it would be unfriendly not to give Ben and Bill credit for coming up with the following:

▶ **Ben:** A lady who married above 'er

▶ **Bill**: Took the gamekeeper on as a lover.
For four hundred pages

▶ **Ben**: In various stages
Of undress, they … well, er, you know, sort of cohabited with each other.*

You can of course play Limericks as a written game – it's fun to do it by post. For other rhyming games that are usually played with paper and pencil, rather than orally, see pages 44–47.

* Reproduced by kind permission of Paul Barnett.

MEMORY GAMES

Word games involving feats of memory do not have to be the exclusive property of the schoolteacher: LAs should take them in hand and claim them as their own! The following three come highly recommended.

This is a variant of the famous Kim's Game, possibly invented by Rudyard Kipling for his novel *Kim* (1901), and certainly made famous by that book. In the original game, Kim looked at a collection of random objects for a short period of time. The display was then covered, and he had to try to recall as many of those objects as possible.

For the logophile version – best with just two or three LAs – you use, instead of an assemblage of random objects, a list of about 20 words randomly chosen from the dictionary by a non-participating LA – the Quizmaster. In fact, they're not quite randomly chosen: if by chance any of them rhyme, or have connected meanings, or have any other characteristic that might make them easier to remember, the offending words are eliminated. The list is read out slowly by the Quizmaster, who then for a few irritating minutes tries as hard as possible to distract the other LAs. At length the contestants go one by one to the Quizmaster and recite as many of the words – in any order – as they can remember. The winner is, obviously, the person who can recall the most words from the list.

If played as a written game this becomes even more challenging, because points are awarded only for words that are correctly spelled.

KIM'S WORD GAME

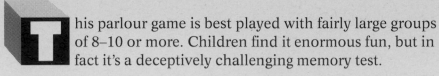**T**his parlour game is best played with fairly large groups of 8–10 or more. Children find it enormous fun, but in fact it's a deceptively challenging memory test.

In principle it's very simple. Each LA prefaces their turn with the words 'I went to market and I bought . . .', then lists all the items that the preceding LAs have said they bought plus one extra, new one. After a little while, obviously, the list gets fairly long and cumbersome! The challenge is not just to remember what everyone else has bought, word-perfect, but to do so in the right order: errors of either type mean you are knocked out of the game. It is easier to play the game if you stick to buying things in alphabetical order – four apples, a bunch of bananas, a bag of carrots for my rabbit, and so on. Play continues until only the winner is left.

One point to watch out for is that, amid the general cries of dismay as someone is knocked out of the game, it is easy for everyone to forget the complete list – or, at least, not to be able to agree what it was, so that the effect is just as disruptive. You can either have a non-participant making notes in the corner or restart the sequence from scratch every time an LA is eliminated.

A typical game might start like this:

▶ **Winston:** 'I went to market and I bought three lemons.'

▶ **Jane:** 'I went to market and I bought three lemons and a punnet of strawberries.'

▶ **Joe:** 'I went to market and I bought three lemons, a punnet of strawberries and a pair of underpants with "I ♥ NEW YORK" printed across their front.'

Note that Joe's stratagem – 'buying' something very silly – is actually quite a good one. Because people will be giggling about it, chances are that later LAs will have trouble remembering Winston's and Jane's 'purchases' as well as the exact wording of Joe's (they'll likely forget the word 'printed').

VARIATIONS

A variant of I Went to Market and I Bought is called I Packed My Bag (or Suitcase) With. The rules are exactly the same, but clearly the types of objects involved will be rather different. Surprisingly, some people who do quite well in one game are much less successful at the other.

A more difficult – but, if the company is right, much funnier – version is Wongo the Alien Packed his Bag With. Of course, here the articles can be as outré as you wish:

▶ seven cans of spray deodorant, one for each armpit
▶ a nosalid fungus from the planet Barg to squeeze at night
▶ the Eiffel Tower (although he had to fold it in half to get it in)
▶ a full set of paloony-scrompers

The game's more difficult because the objects Wongo chose are harder to remember (you can't visualize a paloony-scromper in the same way you can a pair of black patent-leather trousers). It is also often funnier, because a really imaginative company will come up with some hilariously bizarre items.

You can, in fact, play any number of versions of the game. For instance, I Went to a Hollywood Party and I Met: Fred Astaire, Brigitte Bardot, Kevin Costner, Malene Dietrich ... Or you might go to other parties and events and meet pop stars, famous historical characters, villains from books or movies – it depends on what subjects most interest all the LAs who are playing. The possibilities are endless and great fun.

This is guaranteed to be a smash hit at parties, especially when everyone enters into the spirit of the game. It can also cause harmlessly malicious merriment if you use a portable, battery-operated cassette recorder, as described below. However, it's still very well worth playing without any technological eavesdropping.

Beforehand, one LA – usually the host, Hannah – has prepared a story or other piece of prose about 100–200 words long (that's about the length of a decent-sized printed paragraph) or something shorter if young children are joining in. Hannah whispers this story to another LA, Henry, keeping her voice low enough so that no one else can hear what she says – except the microphone of the cassette recorder. She must tell the story slowly and clearly, just once, without any interruptions or hesitations. She then switches off the recorder, and Henry goes with it in pursuit of another LA, Fiona, with whom he repeats the process, reciting the story as near to word-for-word as he can remember it. Fiona then takes the recorder and sets off to find . . . And so on.

Once everyone has had a turn, the last LA, Don, repeats the story out loud – or, at least, his recollection of the version that has just been told to him. Of course, this is likely to be uproariously different from the original that Hannah prepared . . .

The fun of Chinese Whispers lies in the discrepancies between the various versions of the story, so it is best if Hannah makes her original fairly complicated in detail – with several different named characters or locales, for example. At the same time, it can be good to make the plot of the story pretty simple and striking, so that the final version bears at least *some* resemblance to the initial one. It is particularly interesting – and can give rise to much teasing – if you play back the entire tape to discover when, and how, the distortions crept in.

PUZZLES

First, two interesting oral puzzles you can try on your friends and family. For the best effect, don't tell the others that these are actually *word* games: present them merely as puzzles. You'll be amazed at the disparity in the amount of time it can take people of equal intelligence to spot the key to the puzzle.

nnounce to the group that they can have, for example:

▶ a book but not a magazine
▶ eggs but not bacon
▶ a door but not a gate
▶ coffee but not tea

The key is, as you've probably guessed – it's easier to spot this when you can see the words written down – that you can 'have' only things whose names contain a doubled letter ('coffee' has two: 'ff' and 'ee'). You can find countless other related pairs of words with which to play this game – 'queen' and 'king', 'apple' and 'orange', 'jazz' and 'rock' . . . It's a good idea to arm yourself with plenty of examples in case your companions are slow to catch on.

Often enough, the first person or two to spot the secret will, rather than merely announce it, start to join in. Others may follow their example but without having deduced the key, and be baffled when you explain that their selections are ineligible. This can be frustrating for them: end the mystery as soon as you see any signs of tempers becoming frayed.

SINGLES AND DOUBLES

This puzzle is based on the same principle as Alpha–Omega (see page 29): the first letter of a keyword must be the same as the last letter of the preceding keyword.

You need at least two people to be in on the secret. The LAs in the know start a dialogue which is obviously coded in some way; it is up to the others to deduce what the code actually is. For best effect, the keywords should be surrounded by as much 'tinsel' as possible – irrelevant verbiage that draws the puzzlers' attention away from the important item. If you're feeling really mean, you can make a point of pausing before or stressing insignificant words. Here's a possible start to the dialogue:

▶ **You:** I feel hungry. What can I have? I know – an *appl*e. It'll fill up the hole nicely and keep the doctor away.

▶ **Friend:** I'm hungrier than that: I need something really substantial. But I can't be bothered cooking anything too complicated. **E**ggs *and baco*n – that'd take the biscuit!

▶ **You:** Oh, well, if you're planning to start cooking, I think I'll change my mind and have a **n**ut cutlet. I'm a lot hungrier than I thought . . .

PART 2

WRITTEN GAMES

Oral games are ideal for parties, gatherings and journeys, but for the really dedicated logophile they can be no substitute for their written counterparts. Some of the games in this chapter – including classics like **Hangman** and **Consequences** – are not (or need not be) especially difficult. Many of the others, however, are absolute . . . Well, just you wait and see.

You'll find, rubbing shoulders with traditional games, some that are much more recent innovations, like **One-Way Street**, the **Map Game** and **Backronyms**. A few of the games can be adapted for oral play, but otherwise you'll need a pen or pencil and plenty of scrap paper. In addition, some games require a dictionary, printed matter, a cassette recorder or a watch/clock – occasionally all four. You might think of playing some of these games by post, fax or e-mail.

Let's get the ball rolling with a traditional game that appeals to all ages . . .

This venerable parlour game is non-competitive – there is no scoring and no winner. Today it is often overlooked simply because of its antiquity, as if nothing our grandparents played could be fun. Fear not: it's still every bit as entertaining as it ever was – in other words, very. For good measure I've included some more recent variants which you may not have come across. Whichever version you play, it's a good idea to tell LAs in advance to

KEEP IT CLEAN!

The aim of the basic game is to compose a story (or set of stories) according to a particular formula, with each LA, in ignorance of what the others have written, contributing one of a fixed number of steps that go towards the whole story. The results are almost always hilarious, especially when they develop a curious strain of surrealism that has no real equivalent outside the field of word games. In fact, the French Surrealists themselves used to play a variant of this game, which they called *Cadavres Exquis* ('Exquisite Corpses').

The story is written on a single sheet of paper. After each LA has made a contribution, he or she folds over the top of the paper to hide it from the next LA. Once all have had their turn, the sheet is unfolded and the complete story read out. You can opt either for a single story, with one sheet of paper being circulated, or for several simultaneously. For the latter option, give each LA a sheet of paper; after all the first lines have been written, the sheets are circulated one LA to the left and everyone writes second lines; and so on.

The commonest formula for the story is:

▶ **A female character**	A woman's name and/ or brief description
▶ **met a male character**	A man's name and/or brief description
▶ **at a place.**	Name and/or description of the place
▶ **What he did was**	An action
▶ **What she did was**	Another action
▶ **What he said**	A line of dialogue
▶ **What she said**	Another line of dialogue
▶ **What the consequence was**	A plausible – or not so plausible! – outcome of some sort
▶ **What the world said**	Usually a hyper-pious moral

Looking at the formula, you'll understand the injunction to keep things clean! The results of this incoherent teamwork are likely to be sufficiently ribald without the LAs' attempting to make them more so. It is a good idea to write the sequence on a piece of paper that everyone can refer to or else have an LA announce each stage of the story.

VARIATIONS

A stripped-down version of Consequences – one somewhat closer to the Surrealists' *Cadavres Exquis* – has only four steps, the result being a single sentence. These four steps are:

▶ **subject**   either a single word or a phrase – for example, 'Peter', or 'Peter's pet chihuahua', or 'the man with the pimple on his nose'

▶ **verb**   obviously (see immediately below) this must be a transitive verb (that is one which takes an object) – with qualifying adverbs, if desired

▶ **object**   again, either a single word or a phrase

▶ **relative clause** time, place or both

If you want, there can be a final step whereby another LA – still working blind – adds a moral to the story. A typical result might thus be:

▶ Peter's pet chihuahua

▶ loudly kissed

▶ a public lavatory

▶ at three o'clock in the morning in the middle of the Atlantic Ocean.

▶ Not all marriages are made in Heaven.

This Consequences-style game is likely to produce the same blinding oblivion to plausibility that gives both games their surreal charm. The procedure is as before, but this time the first LA, Imran, writes the opening line of a poem. After folding over the top of the sheet of paper, he writes the rhyme-word just below the fold. The next LA, Julia, must compose a second line that rhymes with the first, then another line to start a fresh pair of rhyming lines; when she folds the top of the paper over she likewise notes the rhyme-word for her successor. And so the game proceeds until everyone has had a turn.

Depending on the imagination and creativity of the LAs present, you can end up with outrageous, funny or just silly poems. Most of the amusement comes from the fact that because the LAs only see the word they have to rhyme, the subject matter inevitably changes every few lines resulting in a real nonsense poem. To give you more of an idea of how the poem develops, here is what happened when Sue, Sam and Sid played for the first time (the words they had to rhyme are highlighted):

Sue: It was a day when all was **weird**
Sam: So she took some scissors and cut off his beard.
What a shock! No one knew him **then**
Sid: Five fat pigs ambled through the pen.
What's more, the cow began to **moo**.
Sue: Naturally, this meant the loo!
The seat was loose and **untoward**.
Sam: So spend, spend, spend, if you can't afford.
Christmas cheer and peace to **all**.
Sid: And Humpty Dumpty had a great fall.

It's a good idea to decide on some simple metre for the poem beforehand. Also, as with Consequences proper, it is best if there are as many sheets of paper as there are LAs, so that people aren't sitting around idly for ages awaiting their turn.

Despite its name, this is another Consequences-style word game. It should be done with an odd number of LAs, for reasons that will become obvious. The basic procedure is as before, but this time the first LA, Yvonne, writes down a brief description of an object, or a circumstance, or a proverb, or . . . in short, whatever she likes so long as it's only a few words.

Once Yvonne has finished she passes the sheet of paper, without folding it over, to the next LA, Patrick. Patrick must do his best to make a drawing (or even a little cartoon strip) conveying the same meaning as Yvonne's initial phrase. He then folds the paper so that Yvonne's phrase is hidden from view and passes it to the next LA, Arnie. Arnie has only Patrick's drawing(s) to work from: he must try to reinterpret them into a plausible verbal form. Once he's satisfied, he folds the paper so that Patrick's drawing is no longer visible and passes it to the next LA, who must do a drawing of Arnie's phrase . . .

This is a longer game than either Consequences or Blind Rhyming – the drawing can take a while – but the results are likely to be the funniest of all. Especially interesting is the ingenuity that some LAs display using their limited artistic abilities to convey a phrase. Because of the time factor, you should certainly have as many sheets of paper in circulation as there are LAs.

NOTE: This game is quite hard work so, however entranced you are by the bizarre results of a first round, it's probably best to leave a repeat session for another day.

If Blind Rhyming whetted your appetite for further rhyming games, here is one that comes heartily recommended. *Bouts-rimés*, a game that has been around for over 200 years, relies on the coarse art of writing poetry in reverse.

I'd better explain this. When writing normal verse it is customary to start off with the idea and then work out the poem, including its rhymes, afterwards. In *bouts-rimés* you start off with the scheme of rhyme-words and work backwards from there.

The rhyme-words can be lifted wholesale from an already existing poem, or you can pick a few words at random from a book or newspaper and give each of them the first rhyming word that springs to mind. The latter course is likely to lead to more surreal results, and so is normally the better option. If, though, the LAs decide at the outset that they should at least try to make the poems reasonably sober, then picking rhyme-words from something by Tennyson or Shelley might appeal more.

You need a minimum of two pairs of rhyme-words; the maximum can be however many you want it to be, although 14 is a good choice because then everybody will be producing sonnets. The rhyme-scheme can be whatever you choose – AABB (which means that the first line rhymes with the second, and the third with the fourth), ABAB (where alternate lines rhyme) or ABBA, or something more sophisticated for a longer poem, like a sonnet.

If the rhyme-words given to you were 'test', 'rest', 'howl' and 'foul', you might produce the following:

▶ Put your mind to a novel **test**:
Take your rhymes and compose the **rest**.
Though poets in pain and rage may **howl**,
They can't stop your antics **foul**.

▶ This poem would strong stomachs **test** –
It must be worse than all the **rest**.
Even I, the Poet, **howl**
And wish I could myself cry '**Foul**!'

This is a fine game for playing by post, fax or e-mail. If you do it as a parlour game, make sure you give everybody plenty of time – that way you're likely to get the best results.

This is another rhyming game. Once again it is non-competitive: there is no scoring and no winner – although the laughter and applause should tell you fairly clearly how good your efforts are.

All you have to do is find a serious and preferably famous line of verse – poetry anthologies with indexes of first lines make good sources – and add to it a quick-fire rhyming rejoinder. For example:

▶ Here in this little woodland dell
  Our life in winter will be hell.

Or

▶ Do not go gentle into that good night
  We haven't yet turned on the light!

Or

▶ Earth has not anything to show more fair
  Than Sarah with her bright red hair.

Or

▶ I met a traveller from an antique land.
  I obviously shook him by the hand!

Or there's this yuletime message:

▶ Angels we have heard on high
  Sweetly singing: 'Time to buy!'

This is a pastime for a single LA, although there's no reason why a group shouldn't have fun playing it together and comparing their results.

A pangram is a sentence that contains all 26 letters of the alphabet. It can be of any length but, for our purposes, the shorter the better. The most famous example is the one used for testing typewriters and keyboards:

▶ **The quick brown fox jumps over the lazy dog.**

This uses 35 letters, and is quite a laudable achievement. The sentence makes perfect sense, uses no uncommon words, and involves the duplication of only nine letters. Another celebrated pangram uses only 32:

▶ **Pack my box with five dozen liquor jugs.**

The shorter the target you set yourself, the more difficult it is to compose a pangram. Devising a reasonably plausible pangram of 50 letters or more is quite easy, but – at least to my knowledge – no one has ever succeeded in producing the 'perfect' pangram, a sentence using all 26 letters exactly once. One problem is that short pangrams tend to have to resort to difficult or esoteric words, whereas part of the object is to generate a comprehensible sentence.

A good way to start composing pangrams is first to find words that will 'use up' the less common letters – i.e., 'j', 'q', 'x' and 'z'. For your initial essay, give yourself a pat on the back if you create a pangram in the region of 40–50 letters long. Even after some practice, anything under 40 letters is good and a pangram with fewer than 30 letters is fantastic.

And, if you achieve that perfect 26-letter pangram, grammatically correct and without abbreviations, and it makes a modicum of sense . . .

CONGRATULATIONS!
you're the first in word-game history to do so!

A lipogram is a written text from which one or more letters have deliberately been excluded. The difficulty of composing a lipogram depends on two factors:

▶ **the length of the text**
▶ **the particular letter or letters you have chosen to exclude**

To give you an idea of how far dedicated lipogrammatists are prepared to go, consider the novelist Ernest Vincent Wright, whose *Gadsby* (1939) was written entirely without use of the letter 'e'. Thirty years later the French writer Georges Perec repeated this feat with his novel *La Disparition* (1969); more than that, when Gilbert Adair translated it as *A Void* (1994) – a good punning title, incidentally – he too left out 'e' entirely! Even if you don't plan to read either of these works, you might be entertained by James Thurber's short novel *The Wonderful O* (1957), which is set in a lipogram world.

Omitting the letter 'e' is an especially difficult task, since it is the most commonly used letter in the alphabet (in English). In the first three lines at the top of this page 'e' appears 17 times and 't' 11 times. By contrast, the letters 'j', 'k', 'q' and 'z' do not appear at all. To rewrite even such a short passage without using the letters 'e' and 't' would clearly be no simple task: of the 26 words that appear in those three lines no fewer than 14 – 'written', 'text', 'one', 'more', 'letters', 'have', 'deliberately', 'been', 'excluded', 'the', 'difficulty', 'depends', 'two' and 'factors' – would be unavailable.

This very difficulty is the appeal of The Lipogram Game. It's not for nothing that the 'e'-lipogram, which is obviously the hardest single-letter lipogram, is also the most popular! You have to find synonyms, rewrite phrases and sentences so that they are still readable and 'natural-seeming', express concepts in roundabout ways so as to steer clear of forbidden letters . . . The game itself is non-competitive – although all the LAs are, naturally, striving for glory! The group chooses a piece of prose or poetry and each LA rewrites it without using the letter or letters the group has decided upon. When everyone's finished you compare the results.

CONTINUED... ▶

Just before you dive into the game, it's worth mulling over a few points:

▶ The letter most commonly used in the English language is, as noted, 'e'; it is closely followed by 't' and 'a'. Opinions differ as to the exact order of frequency of the remaining letters but, from commonest to rarest, it is approximately this: 'o', 'i', 'n', 's', 'r', 'h', 'l', 'd', 'c', 'u', 'm', 'f', 'p', 'g', 'w', 'y', 'b', 'v', 'k', 'x', 'j', 'q' and 'z'.

▶ The word most commonly used in the English language is 'the'. Other very common short words, in no particular order, are 'I', 'a', 'of', 'to', 'in', 'and', 'is' and 'that'.

▶ Excluding combinations of two or more very common letters – 'e' and 'a', for example – obviously makes the exercise substantially more difficult.

▶ Rather than choose a letter or letters at random, you can choose a word, all of whose letters must be excluded from the rewritten text. One way of picking your word is to open a book anywhere and take the first word on the page: if it's 'fuzz', for example, you have a comparatively simple task ahead. I once played the game using first 'easy' and then 'hard': not surprisingly, the 'easy' lipogram was harder than the 'hard' one!

After the mental hard work of The Lipogram Game, here is a little mental relief with a pastime that's not so much simple as simple-minded!

Most modern word processors feature a spellcheck facility. If you press the appropriate buttons the program will go through your text highlighting any word which it can't find in its own internal lexicon or dictionary. You have various options when it shows unhappiness with a word – you can tell it to add the word to the lexicon, or to accept the word for now, or to change the word because you have indeed mistyped it. Helpfully, the program gives you a list of suggested alternatives for your intended word. These are based on letter (and sometimes also phonetic) comparisons between your unfamiliar word and the ones in the lexicon – the program has no idea of the *meanings* of any of the words.

It takes only a minute to type in something that's full of obscure spellings – like the first few lines of Chaucer's Prologue to *The Canterbury Tales* – and subject it to the spellcheck, adopting those suggestions you most . . . admire. For example:

> Whan that Aprille with his shoures soote
> The droghte of March hath perced to the roote,
> And bathed every veyne in swich licour,
> Of which vertu engendred is the flour;
> Whan Zephirus eek with his swete breeth
> Inspired hath in every holt and heeth
> The tendre croppes, and the yonge sonne
> Hath in the Ram his halfe cours y-ronne . . .

might become (with appropriate punctuational amendments):

> Whang that April with his sherries Saudi!
> The draught of March hath parched to the roadie,
> And bathed every venue in swish lucre
> Of which verdigris engendered is the flour:
> Wan Zephyrs ache with his swede breath.
> Inspired hath in every holt and hearth,
> The tundra craps, and the yawing sauna
> Hath in the Ram his . . . I've caressed Irene.

On second thoughts, you may prefer the Chaucer . . .

CONTINUED... ▶

Do note that the game is best played on a fairly recently acquired word processor. Systems that have been heavily used tend to have accumulated a pretty large and sophisticated lexicon, because their owners have been adding words here and there. On the other hand, such a lexicon will offer you a far wider diversity of suggestions when it comes across an unfamiliar word.

You could also have fun taking something which contains nonsensical words and seeing what the word processor comes up with. For instance, the first three verses of Lewis Carroll's *Jabberwocky*

> 'Twas brillig, and the slithy toves
> Dis gyre and gimble in the wabe:
> All mimsy were the borogroves,
> And the mome raths outgrabe.
>
> Beware the Jabberwock, my son!
> The jaws that bite, the claws that catch!
> Beware the Jubjub bird, and shun
> The frumious Bandersnatch!
> He took his vorpal sword in hand:
> Long time the manxome foe he sought –
> So rested he by the Tumtum tree,
> And stood awhile in thought.

might become

> Two brisling*, and the slithery toes
> Did gyre and gamble in the wave:
> All missing were the borrowers,
> And the mime rats outgrown.
>
> Beware the Jabberwocky, my son!
> The Java that bite, the claws that catch!
> Beware the Jujube bird, and shun
> The furious Bandersnatch!
>
> He took his verbal sword in hand:
> Long time the Manx cat foe he sought –
> So rested he by the rummy tree,
> And stood awhile in thought.

* By the way, if you didn't know, brisling is another name for sprat!

This pastime – apparently invented by a group of French language enthusiasts in the 1960s – has much the same appeal as Spellcheck Follies. It is easy to do and often, by sheer serendipity, yields intriguingly surreal results – or very funny ones.

First select a short passage from any literary work, poem or essay – the drier, usually, the better – and then substitute each noun with the seventh noun that follows it in your dictionary. By way of example, here is a passage from S.E. Finer's *Comparative Government* (1974):

▶ In its first sense, government denotes the activity or the process of governing, i.e., of exercising a measure of control over others. We use it in this sense when, for example, we say: 'The government of small states is usually easier than the government of large ones.' But government may also be used in a second sense denoting the state of affairs in which this activity or process is to be found – in short a condition of ordered rule.

Once this sober passage falls foul of the crazed word-substituter, however, it becomes:

▶ In its first sentiment, grace denotes the adaptability or the procreation of governing, i.e., of exercising a mediation of convention over others. We use it in this sentiment when, for excise, we say: 'The grace of small steaks is usually easier than the grace of large ones.' But grace may also be used in a second sentiment denoting the steadiness of affixes in which this adaptability or procreation is to be found – in short a conductor of ordered rumination.

The dictionary used here was the *Pocket Oxford* (fifth edition). This game is among the few word pastimes where a small dictionary is preferred: with a large one you are likely to find many of the nouns you substitute are obscure obsoletisms or technical jargon, so that the passage becomes just a wodge of gobbledygook. In less hifalutin nonsense, like the transformed passage above, you are more likely to find intriguing turns of phrase and unexpected connections. The alleged 'grace of steaks' is pleasing, as is the definition of the word 'grace' – especially in this mealtime context – as 'a conductor of ordered rumination'!

VARIATIONS

A variation, perhaps offering a little more flexibility (you are less likely to be substituting words of closely related meanings), is to locate the noun in the dictionary, move 10 pages ahead, say, and use the first noun appearing on that new page.

Of course, your substitutions need not be limited to nouns. Instead you could opt to exchange verbs, adjectives or adverbs, singly or in combination.

The late 20th century may well go down in history as the Age of Acronyms and Initial-Speak: EC, NATO, UN, NERVA, VD, CETI, CERN, ECG, GMT, EST, DC . . . the list goes on seemingly forever. The comparatively few acronyms intelligible to the normal person in the street are but the tip of an iceberg that descends into some very murky depths.

The game of Backronyms has emerged very recently as a waspish response to this mindless proliferation. Its rules are simplicity itself. LAs are allowed to take any half-dozen or more acronyms and abbreviations in everyday use (alternatively, someone can choose an array of acronyms/abbreviations from the dictionary) and invent possible derivations for them. The laurels go to the funniest, most ingenious or – and this is especially noteworthy – most appropriately descriptive. Inspired cheating, such as the use of nonce and portmanteau words, is permitted, and under some local rules actively encouraged. Here are a few examples, with the real derivations in brackets:

▶ **NATO** *(North Atlantic Treaty Organization)*
Nuclear Armaments Terrify Ostländers

▶ **CERN** *(Conseil Européen pour la Recherche Nucléaire – the European Organization for Nuclear Research)*
Chasing Electrons is a Recreation for Numbskulls

▶ **SPR** *(Society for Psychical Research)*
Spooks Photograph Researchers

▶ **THES** *(Times Higher Educational Supplement)*
Top Hegg-'Eads Spoonerize

▶ **HGW** *(Heat-Generated Waste)*
Hot Gases Warmusupmostunwelcomely

You can expand the scope of the game, if you want to, to include proper names, treating them as if they were acronyms/abbreviations. Yes – why not vent your spleen on your least favourite politicians by *backronymming* them? – e.g., 'Mire Afflicts John On Right' or 'Beware Letting Activists Incite Revolution'.

STORY-TELLING GAMES

Most of the written games we've looked at so far involve creative writing rather than problem-solving – we'll be getting to puzzle games, ciphers and the rest later. First, though, why not sample some of the excellent pastimes – ranging from simple to complex – that rely on the oldest literary form of all: story-telling.

No complicated rules here! The LAs are given 10 minutes in which to write a story made up of three-letter words only. LAs then take turns in reading out the results – it can be more fun if you swap stories and read out someone else's. No scoring and thus no winners, of course, but that needn't stop you from handing out prizes.

Although it sounds like an easy game, it is quite difficult putting words together without using 'a' or common two-letter words like 'an', 'at', 'in', 'it', 'of', 'to' and so on. But it's not impossible. You might start:

THE HOT SUN WAS OUT AND SUE RAN OFF THE BUS. SHE HIT HER ARM, BIT HER LIP AND WAS ALL SAD. BUT SHE SAW THE SLY SPY. HIS TOY GUN WAS RED. SAM DID HIS TIE. HOW TO WIN SUE? WHY NOT AIM FOR HER NOW?…

All a load of nonsense!

Or prompt children playing to think about animals. They can't have THE CAT SAT ON THE MAT because of the 'on' but there's nothing wrong with:

THE PET CAT ATE THE RAT. THE HEN HID HER NEW EGG. SHE WAS MAD. WHO WAS THE TOP DOG? THE FOX HAD FUN. THE FAT SOW WAS NOT THE BAD PIG. THE RAM MET THE EWE…

The 10 minutes may initially seem like ages but you soon run out of time. It is a real challenge to make up a story with any sense to it and you'll soon find that you have got to THE END!

THE MÜNCHHAUSEN GAME

This isn't really a word game, but it's too good to be missed out. Karl Friedrich Hieronymus, Baron von Münchhausen (1720–1797), was a real historical personage – a German soldier. He had the habit of exaggerating his own military exploits, and his reputation gave rise to the publication of an anthology of tall tales, *Baron Münchhausen's Narrative of his Marvellous Travels and Campaigns in Russia* (first edition 1785). The most inspired of these were by a renowned archaeologist, Rudolf Erich Raspe (1737-1794), who himself had a somewhat chequered career: thanks to his habitual lightfingeredness, he had to flee his native Germany for England, and then later from England to Ireland, where he died. An excellent movie based on Raspe's stories is *The Adventures of Baron Munchausen* (sic), released in 1989.

After that preamble, here is the very simple game. LAs are given 10 minutes in which to write the tallest tale imaginable, and the results are then read out – with everyone present acting as judges and determining the prizewinner.

The tabloid newspapers have taken the art of headline writing to new extremes of nausea in recent years, and this is your chance to match them! Gone are the days when *Variety* might produce something as deftly aesthetic as

HIX NIX STIX FLIX

to indicate that rural audiences were less than impressed with movies set in non-urban locales, or when the *News of the World*, back in the 1970s, gave us the positively elegiac

NUDIST WELFARE MAN'S MODEL WIFE FELL FOR THE CHINESE HYPNOTIST WHO WORKED IN THE CO-OP BACON FACTORY

Nowadays a more typical headline is

GOTCHA!

For the game of Headline Deadline, one of the LAs in the group – who should not compete in this round – selects a work of literature, preferably a romantic one: Shakespeare's *Romeo and Juliet* and Tolstoy's *Anna Karenina* are two options. The other LAs must imagine this work to be the subject of a tabloid front-page story, and have two minutes in which to devise a headline to go above it. When all the entries are read out, the winner is the LA whose headline is generally agreed to be the most excruciatingly tasteless or badly punned – while yet conveying the gist of the story.

NOTE:

For a longer game, LAs have five or 10 minutes in which to write the accompanying story – to a maximum of about 150 words. The qualities sought for accolade are as in the basic game.

This is another game with simple rules – although playing it is not so simple. LAs have 10 minutes in which to write a 26-word story. Each of the words must begin with a different letter of the alphabet – although local rules may allow 'x' to stand for the prefix 'ex-'. The most amusing or original effort can be proclaimed the winner, although essentially this is a game done just for fun.

To make it more difficult, a theme can be chosen for the story – either by general agreement or by asking a non-LA to think of something – or everyone can write a theme on pieces of paper one of which is then pulled out of a hat or bag at random.

NOTE:

In the standard version of The Alphabet Story it doesn't matter which order you use the 26 letters of the alphabet so long as each of them starts one of the 26 words. More advanced LAs can elect to use the 26 letters in their proper alphabetical sequence. You can consider yourself a pretty sophisticated logophile if you pull off this feat!

U sing a dictionary or other piece of printed matter as a source, 15 words are selected at random: they must consist of five nouns, five verbs and five words of other types – adjectives or adverbs, depending on what turns up. LAs then have 10 minutes in which to concoct a story that uses all 15 words (plus other words, of course), preferably in the order in which they have been chosen.

Another way for the words to be selected is for each LA to write out the required number of different words on small pieces of paper. They should put all the nouns together in one bag, the verbs into another and so on, give all the paper slips a good mix so that they are well jumbled, and then pick words out of each bag in turn. To prevent any cheating, if you are playing by the rules that the story should contain the words in the order in which they were picked, then one LA should make a note of who picks out which words and in what sequence.

Imagine if it had been not Edgar Rice Burroughs but William S. Burroughs (author of *The Naked Lunch*, *Junkie*, *Queer*, *The Soft Machine* and other novels you might not necessarily pick as your Mum's Christmas present) who wrote the Tarzan novels. What would the results have been like? Or what if Raymond Chandler rather than Beatrix Potter had written the Peter Rabbit stories?

Such mismatchings are the basis of this game. Either all the LAs are asked to match a specified writer with a work by another novelist, or LAs can choose their own pairing – it doesn't really matter, because the point of this pastime is pure pleasure rather than any sort of competition. Either way, however, the LAs are given 10–15 minutes in which to produce an extract from the hypothetical work.

Some years ago, playing the game William S. Burroughs's Tarzan, the well-known fantasy writer Colin Greenland produced an extract from *The Lord of the Rings* (in reality by J.R.R. Tolkein) as if it had been written by A.A. Milne (author of *Winnie-the-Pooh*):*

It was a sunny Thursday morning in the forest. The birds were birding, the orcs were orcing, and Rabbit was off somewhere doing the sort of thoughtful things that Rabbit does on a Thursday morning.

Christopher Randalf, Froodo and Samlet were walking along talking of this and that. Christopher Randalf was singing a song in the High Elvish tongue, and Samlet was running along behind squeaking in the Even Higher Elvish tongue, and Froodo was wondering if it was time for elevenses yet, and if not, whether it would be a good idea to have a little something beforehand, just to be on the safe side, and he had almost decided that it was, when something occurred to him.

'Christopher Randalf,' said Froodo.

'Yes, Froodo,' said Christopher Randalf.

'This expotition,' said Froodo, 'which we're going on. What did you say it was, that we're expoting to?'

'To the Crack of Doom,' said Christopher Randalf.

'Oh,' said Froodo.

He stumped along a little farther, Samlet scurrying at his heels and making small breathless going-on-an-expotition-to-the-Crack-of-Doom-on-a-Thursday-morning noises.

Froodo stopped. He turned and looked at Samlet. He looked at the bulging red spotted handkerchief Samlet was carrying on a stick over his shoulder.

'Samlet,' he said.

'Yes, Froodo,' squeaked Samlet.

'Samlet, I have been thinking,' said Froodo. 'I have been thinking, and what I have thought is this. I think,' said Froodo, scratching his ears with one paw, 'that you should carry the Ring, and let me carry the Provisions.'

'Froodo,' said Christopher Randalf sternly. '*You* must carry the Ring, because you are the Ring Carrier.'

'Oh,' said Froodo. 'Bother.'

* Reproduced by kind permission of Colin Greenland.

There are two popular versions of this game, one of which requires you – or whoever is hosting the session – to do a fair amount of preparation in advance. In the other, the LAs all do the preparation together so that it becomes part of the game. I'll assume you're playing the latter version; if you'd prefer the former then your responsibilities will be obvious from this explanation.

The idea of the game is to compose stories from randomly selected elements. You can choose the number and nature of these yourself, but a typical selection (with examples where applicable) would be:

▶ **location**
an old castle, a railway compartment, an artist's studio, the centre of the earth . . .

▶ **characters**
a group of escaped convicts, a deranged robot, two truanting children . . .

▶ **period**
the Age of the Dinosaurs, the late 18th century, six months ago, AD50, some time in the future . . .

▶ **circumstances**
walking in the forest, driving down the road, arguing, surmounting Everest . . .

▶ **time of day**

▶ **style of dress**
blue jeans, heavy winter clothing, nothing, military uniforms . . .

▶ **weather**
stormy, very hot and still, freezing cold, gales and hurricanes . . .

▶ **events**
a burglary, falling in love, being locked in the public library overnight, winning the National Lottery . . .

Each LA (or each team – this game can be played in groups) has the same number of scraps of paper as there are categories. On each scrap the LA writes down an appropriate story element. The scraps are then collected up into piles, one pile per category, and the piles are thoroughly shuffled. The LAs are given one scrap from each pile and, from the randomly assorted story elements they now have, must concoct their tale. Clearly imagination, ingenuity and humour are the qualities being sought, although there is no scoring and no winner.

Of course, LAs may add further elements of their own invention – their tale isn't limited to the ones they've been given. But all of the stated elements must be used centrally. A time limit of 10–15 minutes is reasonable, although you may find the stories are better if people are given longer. When everyone's finished, the stories can be read out by either their individual authors or a single person elected by the company.

VARIATIONS

▶ The Radio Play Game

This is best for a group of about half a dozen: any more and the result is chaotic; any fewer and the result tends to be a bit thin. You need a cassette recorder, a blank tape, and as few inhibitions as possible.

Each LA has two slips of paper, on one of which must be written the details (including name) of a character, on the other the setting for a scene. LAs can be as minimalist or as expansive as they wish about their invented characters. It's a good idea, though, if they give a reasonable amount of detail about the setting: 'a dark night' is not nearly as good as 'a dark night on the Yorkshire moors with the rain pouring down, moments after everyone has discovered the pub they've been tramping towards all day has just shut'.

The character-slips are shuffled and dealt out: LAs must perform as the character Fate has allocated to them. The scene-slips are likewise shuffled: whatever order they finish up in is the order of scenes in the radio play the company will now present. Leaving as little time for thought as possible, switch on the cassette recorder (no later stopping and starting), sound a fanfare of trumpets, and prepare for a dramatic presentation the like of which you've never heard before. And that's no lie.

You can do without the recorder if you want, but you'll kick yourself later if you have no permanent record of a performance that was particularly fine and/or dreadful! Of course, in this context those two adjectives are roughly synonymous . . .

One person starts this game by drawing a previously agreed number of letters of the alphabet – 10–15 is best – from a bag. Alternatively, instead of having to prepare the letters on scraps of paper, they can be chosen by stabbing a pencil at a sheet of newspaper. The letters are recorded by the company as they are drawn. The LAs then have 10 minutes in which to concoct a meaningful telegram using words that each start with one of those letters, used in order; all the letters must be used. Not counted as part of the wordage are the conventional punctuations used in telegrams – STOP, QUERY, etc. – and these can be inserted wherever the LA sees fit. The first word can be the name of the addressee and the last word that of the sender.

As with most other story-telling games, the results are read out at the end, and kudos is given to the composer of the most realistic, bizarre, ingenious, imaginative or just plain funny communiqué.

This is a rather unusual story-telling game – or, at least, it produces a story written in a rather odd narrative form. You require a pen and paper, a little imagination and, ideally, a slightly – or very – twisted sense of logic.

One LA thinks of a conditional phrase and writes it down: it could be 'If I have another cup of coffee…'. At the same time, another LA is, independently, writing down a plausible consequence of something or other – for example, '… the President will sneeze'. The conditional and the consequence are then read out, and with luck will be totally unrelated to each other. (If by chance they seem a bit too plausible, jettison them and start again.) Each LA must then, within a set time (10 minutes, say), attempt to link the two phrases by means of a chain of logically defensible 'if . . . will' statements.

Here's an example of how those two phrases might be linked:

▶ If I have another cup of coffee, I won't sleep tonight.

▶ If I don't sleep tonight, I'll be tired tomorrow.

▶ If I'm tired tomorrow, I'll be less immune to germs.

▶ If I'm less immune to germs, I'm likely to catch a cold.

▶ If I catch a cold, I'll give it to everyone at the office.

▶ If I give it to everyone at the office, the whole board will catch it.

▶ If the whole board catches it, the shareholders will catch it.

▶ If the shareholders catch it, the bank staff will catch it.

▶ If the bank staff catch it, the nation's financiers will catch it.

▶ If the nation's financiers catch it . . .

The chain is getting pretty tedious by now. Its obvious end-point is:

▶ And if the President catches it, the President will sneeze.

Certainly you will expect more imaginative offerings than this from your highly articulate and logically flexible friends! Indeed, while there are no prizes for this game, the public accolade usually goes to the most imaginative solution – although neat, short, deftly logical solutions may be preferred on the grounds of elegance:

▶ If I have another cup of coffee, I won't sleep tonight.

▶ If I don't sleep tonight, I'm going to be so ratty tomorrow that I'll take the bomb I've been developing in my secret germ-warfare project and throw it at the President.

▶ And if the President catches it, the President will sneeze.

CATEGORY GAMES

This description covers many different games, each of which is open to countless variations. There is only room in this book for the basic game and a few of my personal favourites. With these as examples you should be able to devise extra ones for yourself.

The principle of all of them is that you start with a key letter or letters, and must find words beginning with the letter(s) concerned. Most of the games are timed; those involving grids may instead end when the first LA completes the grid or when everyone starts swearing and gives up.

The basic game can be played with any number of LAs from two upwards. LAs take turns choosing categories – artists, seas, US cities, French kings, etc. – until they have a suitable number (somewhere in the region of 5–10). Each LA writes down the list of categories on a sheet of paper, and then is ready to begin the game.

At the start of each round somebody calls out a letter at random – you could open a book in the middle and use the first letter on the page. LAs must within a fixed period (e.g., 10 minutes – but 1 minute per category is a good rule of thumb) write down in each of the categories as many words or names as they can think of that start with the chosen letter.

At the end of the round the results are compared and the scoring begins. There are various scoring systems, but the best is probably to allow 0 points for (i.e., disqualify) any entry that is generally agreed to be invalid ('No, Hamish, Glasgow is not the capital of Scotland . . .'), 1 point for a valid entry that appears also on someone else's list, and 2 points for a valid entry that no one else has registered.

Some categories are by their nature of limited extent – e.g., there are 50 US states – so extra points can be given to LAs who produce complete sets. Generally, however, it is a good idea to limit the number of entries in each category to something like 10–15, thereby reducing the impact of specialist knowledge. Otherwise you may find, for example, a medical student rattling off the names of 40 or 50 nauseating conditions that might as well be Greek.

NOTE:

You won't have any trouble finding categories for this game, but here are a few slightly unusual ones you might like to try:

► irregular verbs (e.g., the verb 'to be')
► palindromic words (i.e., words which read the same backwards and forwards e.g., 'level')
► words without vowels (e.g., 'pygmy')
► 'false friends' – i.e., English words similar to words in another language but in fact of different meaning (e.g., 'chat' and French 'chat')
► onomatopoeic words (i.e., words which sound like the noise they describe e.g., 'plop' or 'buzz')
► irregular plurals (e.g., 'conundra')
► experts (e.g., 'thanatologist')
► young animals (e.g., 'cub')
► male animals (e.g., 'bull')
► female animals (e.g., 'vixen')
► animal groups (e.g., an 'unkindness' of ravens)
► legal terms (e.g., 'primogeniture')
► eponyms (e.g., 'boycott')
► 'arena words' – i.e., words with the same vowel-consonant-vowel-consonant-vowel structure as 'arena' (e.g., 'okapi')
► 'double-or-nothing words' – i.e., words with the same vowel at least

VARIATIONS

Young children, with their inevitably limited knowledge and vocabulary, can find Categories a little too depressingly demanding. They might prefer the far simpler, but similar, game called

► *Word Families*

As in the basic game, the group decides on a number of categories and then the LAs have a fixed period to write down as many examples as they can of words or names in those categories. The difference is that the examples don't all have to begin with the same letter of the alphabet. Categories might include animals, fruit, birds, pop stars, types of sport and so on.

THE ALPHABET GAME

This is a sort of flipped version of Categories. LAs write the letters of the alphabet down the left-hand side of their sheet of paper, and then a single category is decided on – you could ask a non-LA to choose a few beforehand. Within a predetermined time limit LAs must try to write down a word or name starting with each letter.

If someone achieves a full house – all 26 letters – before time is up, the round can stop then. Letters like 'x' and 'z' may be a problem in some categories, so you may opt for local rules which omit them. Some people allow the prefix 'ex-' in place of 'x'. If you want to make the game more challenging, you can start with two or more categories and seek suitable entries for all of them.

Scoring is the same as in Categories.

This variation of Categories was reportedly invented by Mrs Guggenheim, wife of one of the millionaires of that name – although which one is unclear. The essential principle is much the same, but the game is now based on a grid.

The LAs, using whatever technique they prefer, choose five categories – for example, countries, fruits, composers, jobs and vegetables. One LA picks a five-letter word at random by opening a book and calling out the first such word he or she sees. I've just done this and my finger fell on the word 'using'. The LAs then make a grid on their sheets of paper accordingly:

	U	S	I	N	G
countries	USA	Spain	India	Nepal	Germany
fruits					
composers					
jobs					
vegetables					

To fill the grid you need to find, for each category, five words beginning 'u', 's', 'i', 'n' and 'g' respectively. I've filled in examples for the first line. The time limit is 10 minutes, or until someone finishes the grid – although this may be impossible (not many vegetables begin with 'u'!). Scoring is as per Categories.

This is a popular version played in France. The LAs agree a number of categories – as few as five, or as many as 15 for a 'jumbo game' – and write them across the top of their sheets of paper. Someone chooses a letter at random and, within a very short time limit (1–2 minutes), LAs must try to find words starting with that letter to match each category. The 'race' element is important: if someone completes the line before time is up, the round stops then.

Repeat the process several times using different letters, and then score as in Categories.

This is played in the same way as Categories. However, rather than using categories it is based on short words that can be used as the beginnings or ends of longer ones. Here are a few examples:

▶ **starters**
imp
disc
counter
inter
can

▶ **finishers**
ship
city
gent
action
test
scent
antic
nation

There are many others. A list of possible 'hidden words' is a word family in itself. If you don't believe me, start counting how many examples there are in this sentence!

QUIZ GAMES

In this section I'm using the word 'quiz' as in the television description 'quiz show'. In these games LAs or teams of LAs generally compete with each other under the aegis of an MC or Quizmaster – who may be one of the LAs chosen by rote.

 version of this game has long been a staple on UK television. The more traditional parlour game described here is in fact much more fun.

Before the game starts each LA is equipped with an adequate supply of slips of paper. For reasons that will become apparent, these should all be identical. Each LA needs also a pen. The Quizmaster, in this case Natalie, has a comprehensive dictionary – this is certainly no game for a concise one. Natalie finds in the dictionary a word obscure enough that no one among the rest of the company has ever come across it; some honesty is required here, although in fact cheats in this game will find themselves bored rigid – and anyway may not win. Words whose derivation is fairly obvious should also be avoided: 'polyonymous' looks impressive, but in any company at least a few LAs will be able to make an approximate guess at its meaning (having several different names).

While Natalie writes down on her slip of paper the true definition of the word, as given in the dictionary, the other LAs do likewise – except that they invent their definitions: writing them in dictionary-speak, making them seem as plausible as possible, but nonsense nevertheless. When everyone is finished the slips of paper are passed to Natalie, who shuffles them and then reads out the various definitions. Once everyone has had a few moments to think she reads them out again, and this time LAs vote for the definitions they believe to be the correct ones.

LAs score 1 point if the definition they vote for is the correct one, and 1 point if another LA votes for their cod definition. It is not the done thing to vote for your own definition. The game is played several times over – the role of Quizmaster can go from LA to LA, or Natalie may choose to retain it for the full session – and the points are added up at the end.

CONTINUED... ▶

Opinions differ as to the best course to take if you want actually to win this game. Short definitions – 2–3 words – can attract votes both because they seem plausibly boring and because, within such a short scope, you're unlikely to betray the fact that this is not authentic dictionary-speak. On the other hand, who wants to be boring, even if victorious? The true definition of the word is likely to be long and labyrinthine – otherwise the word would not be so unfamiliar – and it takes only a little while to acquaint yourself with dictionary-speak. The more improbable your definition, the more likely it is that at least some LAs will vote for it. In addition, genuinely baffled LAs may well vote for a particularly inventive definition on the grounds that it deserves a vote.

VARIATIONS

Alternatively, you could try playing this as 'The Concise Dictionary Game'. Although Natalie draws the word from a large dictionary, as before, she must reduce its definition to three words or fewer, and the same limitation applies to all the cod definitions offered by the LAs. This version has several advantages, notably that less skilled cod definitions are not so immediately recognizable as fakes, making the game more accessible to younger and/or less experienced LAs.

The dictionaries of obscure and outrageous words mentioned on page viii are ideal for this game. Specialist dictionaries can likewise lead to a good game, although of course their use restricts the imaginativeness of the cod definitions that can be offered. *The Dictionary Game Dictionary* (1988), edited by James Cochrane, is useful, although diehard LAs soon become familiar with its contents. *The Complete Word-Finder Crossword Dictionary* (1981), edited by Bruce Wetterau, is particularly useful in that – unlike most crossword dictionaries – it includes (short) definitions. In the UK, *Chambers English Dictionary* is generally your best bet.

This is a flipped – and very much faster – version of The Dictionary Game. The rules are exactly the same except that this time the Quizmaster, Natalie, reads out not the word but the definition. LAs must produce putative words to match the definition. The scoring system is as for the Dictionary Game.

NOTE:

An enjoyable variant that can be introduced to The Dictionary Game, Bluff My Call and The Quotation Game is the Misère Strategy. If you realize after the first couple of rounds that you're doing extremely badly, to the extent that you have so far amassed no points at all, you can opt to go for the prized Norwegian Trophy: getting through the entire session without scoring – as Norway once did in the Eurovision Song Contest! Unlike the rule in the card game Solo, from which the term 'misère' has been borrowed, you do not declare your intention.

Achieving a misère is more difficult than it sounds. Try it.

This variant of The Dictionary Game is based not on a standard dictionary but on a dictionary of quotations. The Quizmaster, still Natalie, looks up an obscure quotation and reads it out to the company. If no one knows its origin, she writes down the name of the author, the subject under discussion and any other circumstantial detail she sees fit to add. Meanwhile the other LAs are inventing similar details – for example,

▶ **That's one small step for a man, one giant leap for mankind**

might just have been spoken by Fred Astaire to Ginger Rogers on the occasion of their first professional performance together.

The slips of paper are collected from all the LAs, and thereafter the procedure is as per The Dictionary Game.

The flipped version can be even more fun. This time Natalie reads out the details – 'Sherlock Holmes said this to Watson at the conclusion of The Hound of the Baskervilles' – but not the actual quotation, plausible versions of which LAs have to supply from their own imaginations. Voting and scoring are, once again, as per The Dictionary Game.

VARIATIONS

▶ First Lines

Here, rather than a dictionary of quotations, Natalie draws upon a collection of books that the members of the company should have read but probably haven't, by authors whose work is well known to all the LAs. Having shown the cover of a book to all concerned, she writes down its first sentence while the other LAs invent something that sounds plausible. The slips of paper are gathered in the usual way, and voting and scoring proceed as per The Dictionary Game. Another variation is to play Last Lines, which is just like First Lines except that the LAs have to think up the last line in a book.

his is a simple game but it's still a classic – perhaps because of its very simplicity.

All you do is take a single word, preferably a longish one, and see how many other words (no proper names, abbreviations or plurals) you can make from its letters, using each of the letters only as many times in a word as it appears in the original. For example, from the word 'English' you could form 'his', 'leg', 'ling', 'sing', 'shine', 'single', 'shingle' . . . but not 'seen', because the letter 'e' appears only once in 'English'.

Traditional starter words are 'Constantinople' (over 500 words possible) and 'metropolitan' (over 300). Words containing all five vowels ('abstemious', 'facetious', etc.) are generally prolific sources, especially if they have a 'y' as well ('abstemiously', 'facetiously', etc.). Alternatively, you could pick a word that suits the occasion of a party, like 'Christmas' (more than 100 words), 'Hogmanay', 'Birthday' or 'Easter' (a remarkably high yield for a six-letter word – try it!). Short phrases like 'New Year' (more than 70 words) may likewise be used as a starter.

WORD POWER

NOTE:

There are various ways you can make Word Power more taxing on the brain:

▶ allow only words of four letters or more

▶ allow only words of three letters or fewer

▶ allow only words with a particular number of letters (e.g., five)

▶ allow only certain categories of words (see page 67 for ideas on categories)

▶ make the game into a version of Pyramids (see page 90), so that you must start with a one-letter word and work up, letter by letter, to make the longest words you can

▶ play One-Way Street (see page 97) instead

This is really a narrowed-down – and hence more difficult – variant of Word Power. Success depends on reasonable geographical knowledge, so you may wish to avoid this game if the group includes a few of the widespread I Hate Geography Brigade. Conversely, for exactly the same reason it's a good game to play with children, especially those who're showing signs of hating geography – perhaps this game will change their minds!

Spin a globe or open an atlas at random and let your finger fall where it will. Find in the immediate vicinity of your finger a place-name of 10–15 letters (or more) or two place-names which, combined, yield the required number of letters; 'Madagascar' might be a good one-word starter, and 'Vietnam/Laos' a reasonable two-word combination. The names can be of cities, countries, areas, mountains, rivers – you name it.

LAs have to find within (say) 10 minutes as many other place-names as they can using the 10–15 letters of the starter name(s). Depending on local rules, you either can include or must exclude place-name spellings that don't appear on English-language maps; as an example, 'Vienna' is certainly acceptable but 'Wien' might not be. When a place-name comes complete with its category – e.g., 'Red Sea' – there is no need to be able to form the category-word as well; in this instance, 'Red' is quite enough, although LAs should add '(Sea)' to their entry in case of later argument. Category-words in themselves – 'range', 'river', 'ocean', etc. – do not qualify.

To score, give LAs one point for each word they form and a bonus point if it is a word that no one else in the group has thought of.

Before the game starts each LA draws a 5 × 5 grid on a sheet of paper (i.e., there are 25 squares in the grid). The Quizmaster, Eleanor, has a bag of letters written on individual pieces of paper (with popular letters like 'a' and 'e' written more than once) – or she may use a book for random letter selection. She draws a total of 25 letters, one by one, calling them out as she does so. Each time Eleanor announces a letter, the LAs write it down onto one of the squares in their grid – wherever they think it might prove most useful. There can be only one letter in any square, and LAs are not allowed to change their minds afterwards about the positioning.

Once all 25 letters have been called out and everybody's grid is full, the LAs must try to find as many three-, four- or five-letter words as they can by reading horizontally or vertically within their grid. If LAs discover more than one word in any column or row they cannot score with both but must choose the longer one. This means that the maximum number of words any LA can register is 10. However, if the same word appears in two different configurations within the grid, it can be counted as two separate words (e.g., if the sequence 'B-I-N' occurs in both top and bottom rows the LA may register the word 'bin' twice). No abbreviations, acronyms or proper nouns are allowed.

A valid three-letter word is worth three points; a valid four-letter word is worth four; and a valid five-letter word is worth six. The LA with the highest total of points wins the round.

NOTE: You can tinker with the basic version of Grids in various ways. You might allow overlapping words to score separately, so that a row reading

▶ **S W A N T**

would yield the words '**swan**', '**wan**', '**want**' and '**ant**'. Or you could allow words that appear diagonally.

The popular UK television game Countdown tests competitors' verbal and numerical skills. Its verbal component – which involves making the longest possible word out of letters chosen at random – has given rise to a number of modern parlour games.

For the basic game, LAs can contest either as teams or singly. Here I'll assume that everyone wants to compete individually. The Quizmaster, David, has a piece of printed material from which he can select random letters. The first LA asks for a letter to be picked, specifying whether it should be a vowel or a consonant. David calls out the letter, and everyone writes it down. The second LA does likewise, again being permitted to ask for a vowel or a consonant; again David calls it out and everyone notes it. This continues until nine letters have been selected, at which point David starts the 30-second countdown. During these 30 seconds the LAs must form the longest word they can using the nine letters, each letter being used once only. The LA who has produced the longest valid word by the deadline is the winner.

In fact, you're likely to want to play several rounds rather than just one. At the end of each round, LAs are awarded the same number of points as there are letters in the words they have produced, but with nine-letter words being awarded 10 points. At the close of the session, all the scores are added up. If two LAs have the same score, the Quizmaster holds a tiebreaker round – or rounds – between those two LAs to determine the outright winner.

This is a sort of portmanteau game: Countdown meets bowling night. The nine 'pins' are nine letters, chosen by the Quizmaster as for the basic game. Your aim is to bowl a 'spare'. (If you don't go bowling, a 'spare' is where you use two balls to demolish all nine pins.) After the letters have been chosen you have five minutes to try to find as many two-word combinations as you can that use all nine letters. Unlike the case in bowling proper, you don't want to score a 'strike-out' (all nine pins with one ball): you need two words in each instance. For every 'spare' you can score with those nine letters you are awarded a point. The LA with the most 'spares' (i.e., points) is the winner.

Imagine you were really lucky with your letters and got

▶ **N A P L A I E S T**

From this you could derive all sort of combinations, of which the following are only a selection:

▶ A + PLAINEST
▶ IN + PALATES
▶ SEA + PLAINT
▶ LEA + PAINTS
▶ PANE + TAILS
▶ PAIN + TALES
▶ PAIN + SLATE
▶ PAIN + STALE
▶ PAIN + STEAL
▶ PAINS + LATE
▶ PAINS + TALE
▶ PAINS + TEAL
▶ PLAIN + SEAT

This variation of Countdown is harder than it looks. LAs are allocated nine letters in the same way as for the basic game. They must form nine words from those letters, each starting with a different letter. If there are any repetitions in the nine-letter set – e.g., the two appearances of 'a' in NAPLAIEST – then two of the words formed must start with the relevant letter. Using NAPLAIEST as an example, you might form the words:

▶ **n**eat

▶ **a**nte

▶ **p**late

▶ **l**ate

▶ **a**spen

▶ **i**sle

▶ **e**ast

▶ **s**pate

▶ **t**ape

The Quizmaster gives the LAs two minutes to find the words. One point is awarded for each word formed, plus a bonus point for any nine-letter word and another bonus point to any LA who manages to form a full nine words.

NOTE:

For an evening's entertainment, try playing Countdown, Bowl-a-'Spare' and Starters one after the other, three times each, to find the overall winner of a set of nine rounds. Alternatively, rather than play the three in strict rotation, you could choose the particular game for each new round by throwing a die, drawing lots or some other method.

So that the games have equal weight, you need to balance their scoring systems:

▶ Countdown
  10 points for a clear winner with the longest word
  3 points each if two or more LAs tie for longest word

▶ Bowl-a-'Spare'
  3 points for every 'spare'

▶ Starters
  no change to the scoring system

This game can be played with the same set-up as Countdown, so David may as well remain our Quizmaster. Using a pin and a page from a newspaper, he produces a pair of two letters (not the letter 'q'). He announces this 'combination' to the LAs who have five minutes in which to find as many words as possible (four letters or more) containing that combination. Bear in mind that

▶ the combination must be inseparable – you are not allowed to put other letters between the two halves of the pair

▶ the order of the two letters must be in the announced sequence

▶ the combination should not be used to start or finish a word

Thus, if the two letters David picked were 'b' and 'l', words like

▶ tablet
▶ ambling
▶ sable
▶ arable
▶ scramble

would qualify for a score, but

▶ obelisk
▶ halberd
▶ block

would not. If any LA finds 10 words before the five-minute time limit is up – easy with some combinations, almost impossible with others – the round is over. LAs receive one point for each word they've found, with the longest word(s) from the group being awarded a bonus two points.

NOTE:

There are three further, increasingly tough levels of Combinations you can try:

▶ **Level 2**
played as for level 1 but using three letters rather than two

▶ **Level 3**
played with three letters, all consonants: LAs are allowed 30 seconds to try to find any valid word at all, scoring 10 points for a word and 15 for the longest from the group

▶ **Championship Level**
played with four letters (consonants and vowels mixed) and scored as for level 3, with a time limit of one minute

Particularly at Championship Level, you will occasionally encounter 'dummy' rounds, in which no LA can find any word that satisfies the conditions. Don't feel inadequate! Just be determined to think up words in the next round.

This is another word-building game that can be played along the same lines as Countdown. The Quizmaster picks out three letters at random, and LAs have 10 minutes in which to find as many words (not proper nouns or abbreviations) as possible containing all three letters. Ah, but it's not quite as simple as that! There are two extra rules:

▶ the letters must appear in each word in the order in which they were picked
▶ every word must start with the first letter that was picked

As a consequence of these two rules, if the letters chosen were 't', 'l' and 't', the words 'talent', 'triplicate', 'tilted' and 'tallest' would qualify for a score but 'title' (letters used in wrong order) and 'stiletto' (doesn't start with a 't') would not.

To score, award LAs one point for every valid word plus a bonus two points for the longest word produced by the group.

VARIATIONS

Riders can be added to the rules of Scaffold to make the game more difficult.

▶ Why not try **Disjointed Scaffold**? This variation stipulates that the three letters cannot appear next to each other. In our example, 'tilted' would no longer score because the 'l' and 't' are adjacent. If playing normal Scaffold and discovering that the three picked letters form a very common combination – like 's', 't' and 'r' – the Quizmaster can abruptly declare that this round is to be played by 'disjointed' rules.

▶ Another alternative is **All-Round Scaffold**, in which words must not only start with the first selected letter but end with the last one: 'talent' and 'tallest' would still be all right but 'triplicate' would be disqualified.

▶ For **Advanced Scaffold**, pick out four letters rather than three. Or you could try your luck with five letters. Or six . . .

T here would we be without this old classic, beloved of children everywhere? You can play it either between two LAs – the traditional method – or work it as a quiz game, with two teams competing against each other under the supervision of a Quizmaster. For the sake of this description I'll assume you've opted for the latter method.

Beforehand the Quizmaster, Charlotte, has chosen a number of words, phrases, well-known quotations, movie titles, book titles, people's names or place-names to be the targets. For each challenge to one or other team she writes on a large sheet of paper, so that everyone can see, the same number of dashes as there are letters in the target, with the words clearly separated. For example, if the target were the story title *The Diamond as Big as the Ritz*, she would write the clue-line as follows:

$$- - - / - - - - - - - / - - / - - - / - - / - - - / - - - -$$

The LAs in the team call out letters they think might appear in the target word(s). If the letter they announce is present in the target, Charlotte writes it in each position it occurs. For example, if they chose 'I', the line of dashes above would become

$$- - - / - I - - - - - / - - / - I - / - - / - - - / - I - -$$

If, however, they have called out a letter that does not appear in the target, she writes it at the side of the sheet of paper (just to remind everyone that it has been tried) and draws the first line (top left) of the diagram below. Every time they call out a correct letter she adds it to the clue-line; every time they get one wrong she adds a line to the 'hanging' diagram. The round ends either when the team correctly guesses the target word(s) or when the diagram is completed. Teams score a point for every line that Charlotte would have to add to complete the pinman.

All other things being equal, it is in fact easier to solve a long target than a short one: 'The Diamond as Big as the Ritz' should not too much trouble a team, whereas 'pyx' or 'syzygy' might give them considerable difficulty.

Local versions differ in detail, but this is the standard diagram used in Hangman.

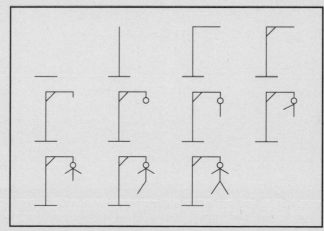

This is an easy game that can be played by any number of LAs – assuming they can all spell: otherwise nasty arguments may break out. If playing the game with children – it is quite educational – make sure that every word called is also spelled out slowly and carefully.

To start with, each LA selects 15 letters at random by picking letters from a newspaper or book. Once everyone is settled, the Quizmaster selects a word randomly from a book or newspaper and calls it out. LAs cross off their list of 15 letters any that appear in the word, with one crossing-off for each letter. (For example, if the word were 'arena' and the letter 'a' appeared three times in an LA's set, the LA could cross it off twice, but only twice.)

The winner is the first LA to cross off the last of his or her letters and shout

'BINGO!'

INVENTIVE PUZZLE GAMES

These word games focus on your ability to solve problems – if necessary by the deployment of lateral thinking. I've called them 'inventive' because creative imagination is another quality the LA will find invaluable. Some of the games are designed to be played competitively; others can be played either solo or in competition with another LA or LAs. All of them are favourites of mine . . .

An acrostic is a poem or riddle in which the first letter of each line spells a word, name or phrase. (In a telestich, conversely, it's the last letter of each line that counts.)

The earliest record of an acrostic dates back to Roman times. Authors have occasionally used acrostics to convey subliminal messages to their readers: alert readers of *The Monster Wheel Affair* (1967) by David McDaniel may have deduced the author's opinion of his publisher, A. A. Wyn, from the fact that the first letters of the chapter-titles read:

▶ **AAWYNISATIGHTWAD**

In about the 1850s a new development of the acrostic appeared: the double acrostic, in which both the first and last letters of the lines form 'message' words. The Acrostic Game, which can be played either solo or in groups, is really a development from the double acrostic.

To start, a word is selected at random. Let's say the word you've chosen is 'great'. Write its letters in a column like this:

G		
R		
E		
A		
T		

CONTINUED... ▶

Now make a second, parallel column by writing the same letters running upwards:

G		T
R		A
E		E
A		R
T		G

The object is to find words that start with a letter in the left-hand column and finish with the respective letter in the right-hand column. For example:

G	ynaecologis	T
R	otund	A
E	ligibl	E
A	viato	R
T	ransectin	G

A point is scored – assuming the words are valid – for each letter appearing between the two columns: the example above would be worth 36 points. The time allowed LAs to find the best possible linkages depends on the length of the original word: as a general rule of thumb, allow three minutes for a five-letter word, four minutes for a six-letter word, five minutes for a seven-letter word, and so on. Proper nouns and abbreviations are, like the keyword itself, disqualified.

What sort of score should you expect to achieve? Much depends on the particular keyword itself, and practice will increase your expectations, but here's a guide for beginners:

	fair	good	excellent
▶ five-letter keywords	25–30	31–39	40+
▶ six-letter keywords	30–39	40–49	50+
▶ seven-letter keywords	40–49	50–59	60+

On this variant of The Acrostic Game the object is to make the links between the two columns as short as possible. Using the example of 'great' again, a good play would be:

G	o	T
R	i	A
E	v	E
A	i	R
T	u	G

The time limit should be short: 45 seconds for a five-letter word, 90 seconds for a six-letter word, and 30 extra seconds for every additional letter thereafter. As in The Acrostic Game, score a point for every letter between the two columns. At the end of a set number of rounds, the winner is the LA with the lowest score.

This game was invented by Lewis Carroll in 1878 and has been popular ever since under various titles, including Word Ladders, Transformations, Transmutations, Doublets, Transitions, Stepwords, Word Chains . . .

It's often forgotten that Carroll was first and foremost a mathematician, writing many books under his real name, Charles Lutwidge Dodgson. You can find a good range of his diversions in *The Magic of Lewis Carroll* (1973) by John Fisher.

Start with two words of equal length; ideally they should be opposites, or related in some way – for example, BOY–MAN, HATE–LOVE, GREAT–SMALL. The object is to work from the first word to the second by producing a series of 'linking' words (no proper nouns or abbreviations), each changed from its predecessor by only one letter. Points are scored for each transformation required, the lower the number of points the better.

To choose an easy example, BOY–MAN, the process could run:

B	O	Y
B	A	Y
B	A	N
M	A	N

There are many 'classic' word links you could try, and many words of diametrically opposite meaning are conveniently blessed with the same number of letters. Or you could have fun taking the two halves of compound words. Here are a few you could practise to get your hand in:

▶ PIG – STY   ▶ FOOT – BALL

▶ CAT – DOG   ▶ BOOK – SHOP

▶ APE – MAN   ▶ WORD – PLAY

▶ HEAD – TAIL   ▶ WHEAT – BREAD

▶ POOR – RICH   ▶ BLACK – WHITE

▶ MORE – LESS   ▶ RIGHT – WRONG

▶ LOSS – GAIN   ▶ NOTES – MUSIC

You should have no trouble thinking of dozens more. To give an indication of what you should aim for, CAT–DOG can be done in three steps (you don't count CAT and DOG themselves), MORE–LESS in four, HEAD–TAIL, PIG–STY, WHEAT–BREAD and APE–MAN in five, and BLACK–WHITE in seven. (It's feasible you may discover a quicker way in some cases.) Otherwise, it's hard to specify targets, since some pairs present far greater problems than others.

Generally the task is easier if the two words have a similar vowel/consonant pattern, like BOY–MAN, which we did easily in two steps. By contrast OLD–NEW, where the two words have different vowel/consonant patterns, will certainly take you many more steps. Normally, however, the longer the word, the more steps needed: most aficionados use words of three to five letters as standard; try pairs of six-letter words if you're really confident about your vocabulary, but don't be too dismayed if you sometimes find the task too difficult. Pairs of seven-letter words are a real test, and the transformation is very often impossible.

NOTE:

For a challenging variation of Lewis Carroll's Word Links, try to 'break your journey on the way'. If you want to make the transformation from LOSS to GAIN, you could decide beforehand that one of your intermediate steps will be EVEN. Here are some other trios you might use:

▶ ONE – SIX – TEN
▶ HEAD – BODY – TAIL
▶ COLD – COOL – WARM
▶ WORD – LINE – PAGE
▶ GRAIN – WHEAT – BREAD
▶ TIRED – SLEEP – DREAM

Ideal for whiling away the time on a long journey, this is essentially a solo game. The aim is to start with a one-letter word and build it up, adding a letter at a time, until you've formed as long a word as possible. You're allowed to scramble the letters of one stage before adding a letter to form the next. In practice, since there are very few one-letter words – just 'a', 'I' and 'o' – you can start also with a Roman numeral ('M', 'D', 'B', 'C', 'L', 'X'), an academic grade ('A', 'B', 'C', 'D', 'E', 'F'), a single-letter scientific symbol (most of the other letters of the alphabet) . . . or, to be honest with yourself, just any single letter that comes to mind.

Here are the first few stages of a pyramid starting with the word 'a':

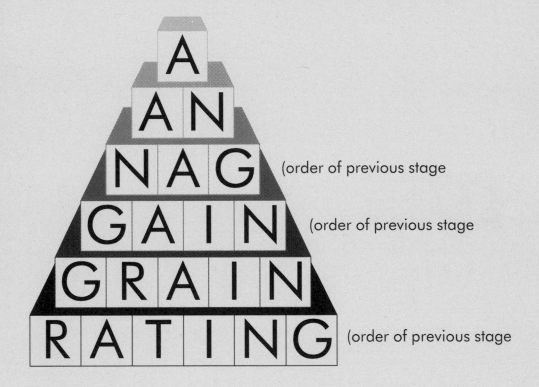

(order of previous stage

(order of previous stage

(order of previous stage

If you can manage a 10-stage pyramid you are doing very well, and a 12-stage pyramid is excellent.

NOTE:

An alternative way to play Pyramids is to turn everything upside down. The rules are much the same as before, but this time you start with a long word and, subtracting one letter each time, try to reduce it to a one-letter word. To make it harder for yourself, disallow Roman numerals, academic grades, etc.

his two-LA game is a sort of free-wheeling version of The Grid-Builder Game. You draw up a 7 × 7, 8 × 8 or 9 × 9 grid (any bigger and the game gets less interesting) on a piece of paper. The first person writes anywhere in the grid a word of at least two letters chosen at random from a book or newspaper. The second LA writes into the grid any other word, but it must intersect the first word, or run alongside it in such a way that new words are formed by the overlap. For example, if the first word played had been

the second LA might write in 'every', forming   or 'aid':

(Note that the two words formed are valid: 'aa' is a type of lava and 'pi' is the ratio between the circumference of a circle and its diameter as well as being a Great alphabet letter – check your dictionary if you don't believe me!)

LAs have a maximum of two minutes to think of a play. Score one point for each letter in a validly played word; in the example above, the LA would receive seven points ('aid' has three letters and 'aa' and 'pi' two each). When LAs can't think of a word that can fit into the grid – doing so becomes more difficult as the grid fills up – they miss a turn. The game ends when both LAs are stuck.

To make the game more difficult decide beforehand on a theme (e.g., geographical names or fictional characters) and allow only words that can be linked to the theme in some way – but let your interpretation err on the

BLOCK SQUARES

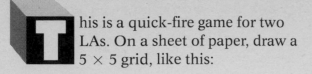

his is a quick-fire game for two LAs. On a sheet of paper, draw a 5 × 5 grid, like this:

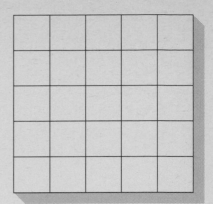

The first LA writes a five-letter word into the grid, running either across or down. For example:

The second LA has 15 seconds in which to add a new five-letter word, ideally intersecting with the first although at this stage it need not. For example:

The first LA responds with another five-letter word, possibly 'inane':

Backwards and forwards the game goes, each LA still being allowed only 15 seconds although of course the problem is becoming progressively harder. At which point – unless you have a bigger vocabulary than I have! – the game is over.

There is no obligation to make one's added words intersect with earlier ones, although in practice it very soon becomes difficult to avoid it. (Any game in which the LAs have simply written down five parallel words is void.) However, a really cunning LA might set out to make as many words as possible run parallel, noticing that he or she should at the last moment be able to form a word crossing all the previous ones. This is a high-risk strategy, and probably best left until you consider yourself an expert at the game.

Decide beforehand the number of games you want to play. The winner of the session can be either the LA who has won most games or the LA who has placed most words (one point per word) – the two systems may not yield the same result. An LA whose addition forms not just a horizontal or vertical word but a diagonal one (this is rare) can be given two bonus points. After the session is over, it's interesting to go back over the games with a dictionary to find out how many other words might have been played. You may get a surprise!

This is another game for two LAs. On a sheet of paper, draw an 11 × 11 grid (or a 7 × 7 grid, or a 9 × 9 grid, or whatever you choose so long as there's an odd number of squares both horizontally and vertically).

The game starts with the first LA writing a one-letter word in the central square – for the purposes of this game Roman numerals and academic grades count as one-letter words. The second LA adds one letter – in any direction except diagonal – to this first entry to form a new word. It is now the turn of the first LA to add a further letter, again to form a new word. Play proceeds with the LAs taking turns to add letters, each time forming a new word or – on occasion – words (no proper nouns).

Any added letter must change the *sense* of the word; for example, if the word 'tone' appears on the grid, you cannot simply add an 's' or a 'd' to form 'tones' or 'toned' – although you could add an 's' at the front to make 'stone'.

At any one time, the same word cannot appear twice in the grid, although the same word may be *played* twice. If this sounds paradoxical, imagine that an LA formed the word 'at', to which was later added an 'e' to make 'ate' or 'eat'. Later on, the word 'at' may validly be formed again elsewhere in the grid. For example, the game could have started with the one-letter word 'o'. The next LA added a 't' to make 'to'. LA 1 added another 't' to form 'tot'. From here the play ran like this:

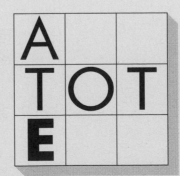

The game ends either when one LA cannot make a play but the other LA can, in which case the other is the winner, or when both LAs find themselves stumped. If you choose the latter option, you must keep score as the game goes along. The scoring system is fairly simple: you allow one point for each letter of the newly formed word – so that, for example, if you added an 'e' to 'fat' to make 'fate' you would score four points. It is possible, however, that the addition of a single letter might form more than one new word, in which case you must add together the total number of letters in both new words to arrive at the LA's score. (If one of those new words is merely a plural or a conjugation the play is valid but the LA does not score for the word concerned.) For example, if the grid looked like

and an LA inserted an 'r' to make

the score would be five: three points for 'art' plus two for 'or'.

This is the lexical cousin of the well-known board game Mastermind®. You've almost certainly played the original – it's a very good game – but in the ensuing description I'll assume that you haven't.

A Codemaker – whom we'll call Catherine – thinks of a five- or six-letter word, writes it down on a piece of paper and folds it away, and tells the Codebreaker – whom we'll call Paul, although in fact there may be a team of Codebreakers – how many letters the word has.

Paul now has a set number of attempts (e.g., 10) in which to try to determine the word Catherine has written down. For each attempt, Paul writes down on a large sheet of paper between them a guessed word, beside which Catherine registers a score: she can award a circle for each letter that is correct and correctly positioned, and a cross for each letter that appears in both her word and Paul's but not in the same position. For example, if her word were **SCHOOL** and Paul had guessed at it being **SOCIAL**, she would mark his attempt like this:

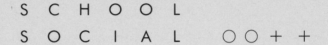

This indicates that Paul's attempt has two correct and correctly placed letters ('s' and 'l') as well as two correct letters that are in the wrong places ('o' and 'c'). Notice that the marking system does not indicate which of Paul's letters are correct.

On the basis of his first attempt, Paul can back a hunch, make a guess or even deduce what might be a better offering. He could, for example, guess that the 's' and 'o' are correctly placed. This means that only two of the other letters in 'social' can be in Catherine's word. A good attempt in this context would be 'soiled', which Catherine scores accordingly:

The game proceeds like this until either Paul's 10 attempts are up or he manages to deduce Catherine's word.

Once you have the hang of Word Mastermind you can think of playing it with longer words. You may find, surprisingly, that you need not increase the number of attempts Paul requires in order to find the answer: the longer the word, the more likely it is that any wild guess of his will produce a score that gives him useful information.

This game can be played either solo or as a quiz game. In the latter version, the Quizmaster picks two words (five letters or more) at random and the LAs write them down. Say the two words are 'March' and 'April'; these would be written down to form a 'one-way street' like this:

M A R C H A P R I L

The LAs are given five minutes in which to find as many as possible words of three or more letters than can be extracted from this combination, reading left to right – not right to left, because this is a one-way street. The two original words, 'March' and 'April', do not count. A few valid words are:

▶ MAP
▶ RAP
▶ HAP
▶ ARCH
▶ MAIL

Remember that

▶ PARCH

is invalid because, in the original combination, the 'p' comes after the other four letters.

LAs score three points for every three-letter word, four for every four-letter word, and so on, with a three-point bonus given to the LA who produces the longest word (but no bonus if two or more LAs tie). Alternatively, you can score two points for each word discovered in direct sequence (e.g., 'hap', 'arch') and one point for each word in indirect sequence (e.g., 'rap', 'mail'), with the bonus as before. You can make both scoring patterns more challenging by awarding points only for words that no one else has discovered.

VARIATION

▶ Two-Way Street

In this version you can discover words reading not only left to right but also right to left. The other rules and the scoring system are as for One-Way Street, but you may want to double the time allowed to the LAs.

CLUE GAMES

Here are a couple of games that depend on the ability to solve crossword-style clues. Not everyone is familiar with the various styles of crossword, so perhaps I'd better give a few introductory notes.

There are two principal types of crossword: plain crosswords and cryptic crosswords. Plain crosswords are based on straightforward clues that usually consist of definitions; for example, the clue 'Capital (5)' might indicate the light (i.e., solution) 'Paris'. Cryptic clues – which are almost unknown in the USA – instead use puns, anagrams and other devices in order to allude to the correct light; a very simple cryptic clue to 'Paris' might be 'Standard is capital! (5)', because 'par' means 'standard', and 'par' + 'is' = 'Paris'. Here are some other examples of cryptic clues:

▶ **Work here and dislike diamonds (6)**
office (a word charade: 'off' + 'ice')

▶ **City has net fixed (6)**
Athens (anagram of 'has net')

▶ **Arrest at end of sentence? (4)**
stop (a pun: 'arrest' means 'stop', and a stop comes at the end of a sentence)

▶ **GGES? (9, 4)**
scrambled eggs (a rebus, 'gges' being the letters of the word 'eggs' scrambled)

▶ **Send Peter out to leaders' locale (4)**
spot (the leaders, or first letters, of 'send', 'Peter', 'out' and 'to')

▶ **See way round river (4)**
spot (in its different meaning of 'see': a street, or 'St', is a way, and 'Po' is a river)

▶ **Mark in baby's potty? (4)**
spot (the word 'in' prompts you to look at the words 'baby'[spot]ty')

▶ **Pastime – don't take the damned thing! (4)**
spot (yet again! – 'pastime' = 'sport'; 'R' is an accepted abbreviation in recipes for 'take', and so the clue hints you should remove the 'r' from 'sport'; and a famous quotation from *Macbeth* is 'Out, damned spot!')

In almost all instances cryptic clues contain a definition part, which states or at least alludes to the correct light, and a cryptic part, from which the solver may in some way or another decrypt the light.

A cryptic clue can be judged by the (apparent) clarity and internal logic of the sentence(s) presented to you, by the wit and ingenuity of the setter, and by its precision – if it leads to several possible answers it's a poor clue. For example, if the light were the word 'essential',

▶ **One cannot do without funny lane sites (9)**

would not be regarded as a very good clue, because 'lane sites' is such an obviously artificial phrase that it could hardly be anything else but an anagram. It does have the virtue, though, that once you've solved it you can write it into the grid with confidence; that is, it's very precise. But a much better effort would be:

▶ **Germans eat before they begin taking in alcoholic liquor – they have to! (9)**

This is equally precise and a much more plausible sentence. (The German for 'to eat' is 'essen'; the first letters of 'taking in alcoholic liquor' are 't', 'i', 'a' and 'l'.)

Seasoned cryptic-crossword solvers can usually recognize almost at once the type of coding that has been used. Beginners may have more difficulty, so here are a few pointers:

▶ clues involving **anagrams** should contain a word or phrase denoting change, movement, error or confusion of some kind; e.g., 'alter', 'crazy', 'mixed-up', 'scrambled', 'all over the place', not to mention 'change', 'movement', 'error' and 'confusion' themselves

▶ **abbreviations** and **acronyms** frequently play a part in the light, classic ones to look out for being 'railway' ('ry' or, in the UK, 'BR'), 'morning' and 'afternoon' ('am' and 'pm'), 'king' and 'take' (both 'r'), 'street' and 'saint' (both 'st', although the latter may be just 's'), 'road' ('rd'), 'beginner' ('L' – for Learner driver), 'quiet' and 'loud' ('p' and 'f'), along with numbers (Roman numerals) and standard symbols for chemical elements, measures, countries, US states, the compass points . . .

▶ whenever a **nationality/language** is mentioned in a clue it is likely that you need to make some simple translation to form an element of the light – so that, for example, 'a French . . .' suggests 'un' or 'une' and 'the French . . .' suggests 'le', 'la' or 'les'

▶ a **pun** is usually indicated by an expression like 'reportedly' or 'we hear'

CONTINUED... ▶

As with all skills, you become better at solving cryptic crosswords the more you practise. All the better UK daily and Sunday newspapers contain cryptic crosswords; some of the tabloids do as well, but their standard is not high – in fact, they can be more difficult to do because the clues are so imprecise and generally poor. Of the dailies, the *Independent*, *Daily Telegraph* and *Times* have a fairly consistently difficult crossword; the *Financial Times* has a good but rather easy crossword; and the difficulty of the crossword in the *Guardian* varies widely with the setters (all of whom are pseudonymous) – running from compilers like Shed, Bunthorne and the brilliantly ingenious Araucaria, who between them produce by far the best crosswords in UK dailies, to the more standard Custos and Rufus.

Most of the UK Sunday broadsheets (as well as the Saturday *Independent*) contain, alongside a standard cryptic crossword, a harder one constructed according to such different principles that perhaps these puzzles should be considered as forming a separate genre. They have no black squares at all, the completed crossword forming a solid grid of letters; there are occasional vertical or horizontal bars to indicate where one word ends and another begins. Moreover, whereas in the standard cryptic crossword it is assumed that most of the lights will form part of a – perhaps very extensive – everyday vocabulary, these regard as fair game any word that appears in a comprehensive dictionary (most specifically recommend the *Chambers English Dictionary*). The challenge they present is thus of a very different nature to that offered by a normal cryptic crossword: armed with the requisite dictionary, you must engage in patient, piecemeal deduction in order to arrive at words you have likely never encountered before (and may never again!).

The best – i.e., most difficult – of these crosswords is the *Observer*'s Azed, followed by the *Sunday Times*'s Mephisto and the *Independent on Sunday*'s Beelzebub. The similar crossword in the Saturday *Independent* colour supplement is of variable standard but often extremely interesting: it always invokes special rules – for example, several lights may be unclued, all referring to a single theme that must be deduced from elements elsewhere within the crossword, or even from beyond it. The other crosswords in this category – and those by the *Guardian* conventional-cryptic setter Araucaria – often likewise invoke special rules.

If you are not a regular cryptic-crossword solver, the delights of Beelzebub and especially Azed lie some way in the future. Your best bet might be to buy a collection of fairly straightforward cryptic crosswords, like the *Observer*'s Everyman (in fact, Custos of the *Guardian*) or the *Financial Times* crosswords. Such books are readily available at most good bookshops in the UK; they can be ordered through larger US bookshops. A considerable advantage of such anthologies is that, if entirely baffled, one can look up the answer in the back and thus learn how to solve similar clues in future.

This game is derived directly from the cryptic crossword. All the LAs in the group select a word at random from a book or newspaper and have five minutes in which to devise and write down a cryptic clue for that word. The clues are then read out (complete with the numbers of letters in the mystery words), so that everyone can write down the full set. The LAs are then given a set time – five minutes for a smallish group, longer for a larger one – in which to try to solve as many of the clues as possible.

The winner is the LA who solves the most clues, with special commendation to anyone who solves all of them. Scoring – as for example one point per clue solved – isn't a good idea, though: there tend to be nasty arguments about the 'correct' answers to some clues!

VARIATION

▶ Oscar Wilde's Cryptic Clue Challenge

This has nothing whatsoever to do with the great Irish playwright except for the fact that the LAs are seeking to emulate him. Any LA chooses a word or phrase at random from a book or newspaper, a *bon mot* from the dictionary of quotations, a famous name or whatever else seems a good idea at the time. Everyone has two minutes in which to devise a corresponding cryptic clue. The winner, if you want to be competitive about this, is the LA who produces the clue generally accepted as the funniest, most ingenious or most tortuous.

This is really a written equivalent of Charades (see page 20). Each LA thinks of a longish word – 10 letters or more – and then breaks it down into shorter ones. LAs in turn devise clues – cryptic or straightforward – to enable the other LAs to deduce those shorter words and hence, eventually, the longer one.

The rules are rather complicated to explain in isolation, so let's take an example. You've chosen the word 'vocabulary' as your mystery word. The first thing you must do is number its letters:

V	O	C	A	B	U	L	A	R	Y
1	2	3	4	5	6	7	8	9	10

From these letters you must make up several smaller words, ensuring that every letter in 'vocabulary' is used at least once. Let's say you decide on the words

▶ **vary** (letters 1, 4, 9 and 10)
▶ **buy** (letters 5, 6 and 10)
▶ **local** (letters 7, 2, 3, 8 and 7)

After telling the other LAs the number of letters in the mystery word, you could clue the shorter words to them as follows:

▶ my 1, 4, 9, 10 is to make a change
▶ my 5, 6, 10 is what people do in a supermarket
▶ my 7, 2, 3, 8, 7 is near your home

Either together or individually the LAs have five minutes (or 10 if you're using cryptic clues) to try to work out the answer. If they are still baffled at the end of this time, you can give them a clue to the mystery word itself:

▶ my whole is what reading dictionaries increases

If this does not lead the other LAs to the answer within a further two minutes or so, the round is over and – after you've explained your reasoning – another LA sets the charade for a new word.

Once you have the hang of the basic game you could think of extending it to book or movie titles, names of famous people, proverbs and so on.

PART 3

PUZZLE-SETTERS' CORNER

Some people make a career out of puzzle-setting, notably crossword compilers, the devisers of the 'brain teasers' you often see in newspapers and magazines, and the marketing employees who make up the quizzes and other puzzles sometimes used for promotional competitions. But everyone can enjoy themselves by engaging in puzzle-setting as a pastime.

Aside from at parties and gatherings of friends, the commonest medium of amateur puzzle-setting is by post – although e-mail word-gaming is developing rapidly – and so for most of this section of the book I've assumed that this is what you'll be doing. Most of these games involve cryptography (codes of some sort) in one form or another, so I've concentrated on this. Other traditional games for playing by post include *Bouts-Rimés* (see page 46), Word Power (see page 75), Word Charades (see page 102) and home-made crosswords.

First, though, a word-based game (definitely not played by post!) that is often included at parties, and fairly elaborate parties at that. It's that old country-house classic the Treasure Hunt …

Somewhere in the house or – let's go the whole hog – the surrounding estate there is a 'treasure'. LAs can find the 'treasure' only by following a set of individually discovered clues distributed around the area such that each clue leads to the next, with the 'treasure' lying at the end of the sequence. At the outset the LAs are given the first clue to start them on their way.

The clues are usually presented as a riddle of some form. This can be a cryptic clue (see page 98), an acrostic (see page 108) or some other encryption of the basic information. The information about the next clue might be, for example, the title of a book into which it has been tucked, a container under which it has been laid, or even the name of a person who will recite the new clue if asked to do so. So typical answers could be:

▶ *Great Expectations*
▶ red biscuit tin
▶ Joanna Ryde
▶ privet hedge

Somewhere in the region of 7–10 clues is about right for the average Treasure Hunt: any fewer and the game will be over too soon (and will seem hardly worth all the trouble you took devising it!), any more and you run the risk of LAs' mystification degenerating into boredom. The 'treasure' itself need be nothing much – indeed, it's probably best if it's worthless. A chocolate bar, a penny, a note wishing the winners a million dollars' worth of good luck . . .

This is a fairly easy way to hide a message, although at the same time it's quite time-consuming. For reasons that will become obvious, your message must have an even number of letters. Let's say you want to tell a friend that

▶ I WISH YOU A VERY HAPPY BIRTHDAY

First of all, divide up your paper into five columns. Your friend has to write words into columns 1, 3 and 5 in order to derive letters that, when put into columns 2 and 4, will spell out your message. The numbers in columns 1, 3 and 5 relate to the set of clues you've supplied. The dashes in those columns tell your friend how many letters there are in each of the words.

Imagine the words in a single row. Whatever the word in column 1 might be, the word in column 3 is made up of an anagram of its letters *plus one extra letter*. This letter is to be written into the appropriate space in column 2. Likewise, the word in column 5 is formed from a jumble of the column-3 word's letters plus an extra one, which is to be written into column 4. Let's look at an example:

1	2	3	4	5
later	i	retail	l	literal

The letters of the word 'later', jumbled together and with the addition of the letter 'i', form 'retail'. Likewise, the letters of 'retail' plus the letter 'l' can be used to make 'literal'.

To compile a Laddergram, first write your message into columns 2 and 4 to remind yourself which extra letter you will need to add for each of the transformations. Next concentrate on filling in column 5, bearing in mind that each word in that column must contain the two letters from columns 2 and 4 in its row. To give yourself plenty of flexibility when composing the shorter words in columns 3 and 1, try to make sure that the other letters in your column-5 word are fairly common ones, like 'e', 'a' and 's'. For similar reasons, it's a good idea to use pencil rather than pen, in case you discover difficulties forming words for columns 1 and 3 from your column-5 word and decide to start that row over again.

In the birthday message we chose, the letters in columns 2 and 4 in the first row prove to be 'I' and 'h', so a good choice of column-5 word might be 'Chinese'.

CONTINUED... ▶

Working back along the row, the word for column 3 must therefore be an anagram of 'Cinese': 'nieces', for example.

The word for column 1 must be made up from the letters of 'neces': your obvious choice is 'scene'.

Once you've completed all the rows, draw up your Laddergram again but, of course, leaving out the words and letters. In their place put numbers for the clues and dashes to indicate word-lengths. This is the version of the Laddergram you will send to your friend, once you have devised all the clues. Those clues can be of any type you wish (straightforward definitions and synonyms, words missed from phrases or titles or quotations, examples of a general nature, or cryptic clues of the type discussed on pages 98–100), and as easy or as difficult as you think it fair to inflict on your friend.

The Laddergram you put in the post could look like this:

1	- - - - -	—	2	- - - - - -	—	3	- - - - - -	—
4	- - -	—	5	- - - -	—	6	- - - - -	—
7	- - - -	—	8	- - - - -	—	9	- - - - - -	—
10	- - -	—	11	- - - -	—	12	- - - - -	—
13	- - -	—	14	- - - -	—	15	- - - - -	—
16	- - - -	—	17	- - - - -	—	18	- - - - - -	—
19	- -	—	20	- - -	—	21	- - - -	—
22	- - -	—	23	- - - -	—	24	- - - - -	—
25	- - -	—	26	- - - -	—	27	- - - - -	—
28	- - -	—	29	- - - -	—	30	- - - - -	—
31	- - -	—	32	- - - -	—	33	- - - - -	—
34	- - -	—	35	- - -	—	36	- - - - -	—
37	- - - -	—	38	- - - - -	—	39	- - - - - -	—

1 Don't make one when you see this!
2 Female relatives
3 Type of chequers
4 Eggy drink
5 Formal dress
6 Horse-drawn vehicle
7 Unwise
8 They're sometimes split
9 Small local division
10 It's sometimes stopped
11 Type
12 Tennis, for example
13 Depressed
14 Rush
15 Unethical, as a deal may be
16 Actual
17 Type of bird or days
18 A cereal (with sugar?)
19 *Darkness – – Noon*

20 Food grain
21 Not a lot
22 Body part
23 Adhesive
24 Oatmeal dish
25 Formal letter's addressee
26 Tunes
27 – – – – way or – – – – well
28 MGM lion
29 It's all you need

30 Mean abode
31 Weapon
32 Equine female
33 'I have a – – – – –'
34 Immerse briefly
35 Leak, as a tap
36 Quick
37 Peer
38 Type of race
39 Annually

Your friend will doubtless be delighted to spend hours or even days of effort to reveal your profound message! Here's the completed Laddergram:

1	SCENE'	I'	2	NIECES'	H'	3	CHINESE'
4	NOG'	W'	5	GOWN'	A'	6	WAGON'
7	RASH'	I'	8	HAIRS'	P'	9	PARISH'
10	ROT'	S'	11	SORT'	P'	12	SPORT'
13	SAD'	H'	14	DASH'	Y'	15	SHADY'
16	REAL'	Y'	17	EARLY'	B'	18	BARLEY'
19	AT'	O'	20	OAT'	I'	21	IOTA'
22	LEG'	U'	23	GLUE'	R'	24	GRUEL'
25	SIR'	A'	26	AIRS'	T'	27	STAIR'
28	LEO'	V'	29	LOVE'	H'	30	HOVEL'
31	ARM'	E'	32	MARE'	D'	33	DREAM'
34	DIP'	R'	35	DRIP'	A'	36	RAPID'
37	EARL	Y	38	RELAY	Y	39	YEARLY

It doesn't take much ingenuity to adapt the standard Acrostic or Double Acrostic (discussed opposite) to form a puzzle message. Again, you need to clue words which have to be laid out in a certain way so that the message can be revealed. If your message were a simple 'Happy Birthday' you could send your friend an Acrostic like this.

1	- - - - -'	President Truman, to friends'
2	- - - - -'	Calculating viper?'
3	- - - - -'	Serenity'
4	- - - - -'	What evidence can produce'
5	- - - - -'	Loretta or Robert'
6	- - - - -'	First move in Pool'
7	- - - - -'	Perfect'
8	- - - - -'	Circular'
9	- - - - -'	Freshwater fish'
10	- - - - -'	Ivy's friend'
11	- - - - -'	Milking spot'
12	- - - - -'	The Big - - - - -'
13	- - - - -	Fermenting agent

Although all the words in this Acrostic are five letters long, you don't need to follow this rule – in fact, the words you use can be of all different lengths. Your friend should be able to solve the puzzle to find:

1	HARRY'
2	ADDER'
3	PEACE'
4	PROOF'
5	YOUNG'
6	BREAK'
7	IDEAL'
8	ROUND'
9	TROUT'
10	HOLLY'
11	DAIRY'
12	APPLE'
13	YEAST

Alternatively, you can set out the Acrostic as a grid, with the answers to the clues running downwards and the message running across the tops of the columns – which is the way we'll do it for Double Acrostics.

Double Acrostic is like an Acrostic except that not only the first letter but also the last letter of each line contributes to the hidden message. The same principle is easily adaptable to the compiling of a puzzle message. In order to discover the message, either:

▶ your friend must solve a set of clues, as for an Acrostic

▶ you supply, without any clues, a grid of words whose first and last letters are missing, so that your friend has to deduce the full words and hence the message.

In the latter instance you might send something like this:

_'	_'	_'	_'	_'	_'	_'	_'	_'
O'	S'	A'	O'	A'	A'	T'	O'	O'
O'	C'	N'	L'	C'	N'	A'	D'	F'
K'	E'	D'	I'	H'	J'	L'	E'	–
A'	N'	–	C'	–	–	–	–	
–	–		–					

Eventually your friend should realize that the words needed to complete the grid are 'hookah', 'ascend', 'panda', 'policy', 'yacht', 'banjo', 'Italy', 'rodeo' and 'tofu', so that your message is disclosed:

H'	A'	P'	P'	Y'	B'	I'	R'	T'
O'	S'	A'	O'	A'	A'	T'	O'	O'
O'	C'	N'	L'	C'	N'	A'	D'	F'
K'	E'	D'	I'	H'	J'	L'	E'	
A'	N'		C'					
H	**D**	**A**	**Y**	**T**	**O**	**Y**	**O**	**U**

CODES AND CIPHERS

The allied arts of creating and breaking codes seem to be almost as old as writing itself. Certainly since the days of Ancient Greece people have been using codes to send secret messages, whether to protect confidential matters of state or simply to entertain each other. Countless codes and ciphers have been devised – it would be impossible to reproduce here even so much as a comprehensive list of them. There are various books on the subject you can read if you'd like more information: Martin Gardner's Codes, Ciphers and Secret Writing (1972) can be recommended.

Let's look briefly at six classic ciphers.

This is very easy. The coded message takes the form of a set of numbers. The encrypter has represented each letter of the alphabet by a number, from A = 1 to Z = 26. All the decrypter has to do is to number the letters of the alphabet and then translate the message back from numbers into letters.

Of course, there's no reason why the numbers should follow the order A = 1, B = 2, C = 3 through to Z = 26. The numerical order can be quite different from the alphabetic one, just so long as the decrypter knows what the chosen order is. Something else within the message may supply the decrypter with the information necessary to determine how the letters have been numbered, and thus to translate the message as before. To take a simple example, you and your friend may have decided beforehand that the date of the communication will always serve as the key, the months January to December being numbered from one to twelve (the numbers being spelled out like that). Imagine you've dated your message 6 November. Your friend writes out the alphabet and then above it the date, starting to number the letters after the date has been written and continuing after Z with A, B, C, etc.:

S	I	X	E	L	E	V	E	N																	
A	B	C	D	E	F	G	H	I	J	K	L	M	N	O	P	Q	R	S	T	U	V	W	X	Y	Z
18	19	20	21	22	23	24	25	26	1	2	3	4	5	6	7	8	9	10	11	12	13	14	15	16	17

Because the number of letters 'displaced' by the date changes almost every day, so does the code, which is reasonably difficult to crack.

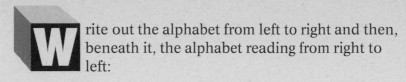

Write out the alphabet from left to right and then, beneath it, the alphabet reading from right to left:

A	B	C	D	E	F	G	H	I	J	K	L	M	N	O	P	Q	R	S	T	U	V	W	X	Y	Z
Z	Y	X	W	V	U	T	S	R	Q	P	O	N	M	L	K	J	I	H	G	F	E	D	C	B	A

To code your message, read off each of its letters along the top line and substitute with the corresponding letter from the lower line: A = Z, B = Y, C = X and so forth. A message reading 'Happy Birthday' thereby becomes 'Szkkb Yrigswzb'. Your friend may think you've sent your greeting in Polish!

Another code involves displacing the letters of the alphabet one, two, three or any number of places forwards or backwards. For example, if you'd decided to displace them three steps backwards, your index to the coded message would look like this:

A	B	C	D	E	F	G	H	I	J	K	L	M	N	O	P	Q	R	S	T	U	V	W	X	Y	Z
X	Y	Z	A	B	C	D	E	F	G	H	I	J	K	L	M	N	O	P	Q	R	S	T	U	V	W

'Happy Birthday' thus becomes 'Exmmv Yfoqeaxv' – could this be Greek?

THE PIGPEN CIPHER

This gets its name because, before coding, the letters are laid out in grids such that they are separated from each other by lines, like pigs in a pen. The precise layout of the grids is something that you and your friend must decide between yourselves beforehand. A typical layout would look like this:

Using these grids, the coded version of the message 'Happy Birthday' would look like this:

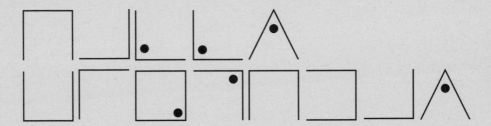

You can devise your own grids, making sure always that the symbol derived from them for any particular letter is, within the code, unique to that letter. Also, of course, there's no need to arrange the letters within the grids in the same order as I've put them here. Play around with all the permutations as much as you and your friend wish: the end result will be a code that is extremely difficult for anyone else to crack.

Decide on a six-, seven-, or eight- letter keyword. You can choose it at random from a book or newspaper if you wish, but do make sure that it contains no repeated letters: the word 'ginger', for example, would be disqualified because of the repetition of the letter 'g'.

Let's choose 'splinter' as our keyword: it has eight letters, all different. Write out the letters of the alphabet and then under them write the word 'splinter' followed by the rest of the letters of the alphabet in their normal sequence but omitting the letters 's', 'p', 'l', 'i', 'n', 't', 'e' and 'r':

A	B	C	D	E	F	G	H	I	J	K	L	M	N	O	P	Q	R	S	T	U	V	W	X	Y	Z
S	P	L	I	N	T	E	R	A	B	C	D	F	G	H	J	K	M	O	Q	U	V	W	X	Y	Z

In this code your 'Happy Birthday' message becomes 'Rsjjy Pamqrisy'. This could possibly be something like Hungarian . . . Unless your friend catches on soon to the fact that you are writing in code, he or she is going to imagine you've become a most impressive polyglot!

This is generally reckoned to be the hardest to crack of the six ciphers I describe here. To begin with you must select a keyword on exactly the same principles as for the Keyword Code: six, seven or eight letters, with no duplications. We'll retain the word 'splinter'.

The letters of the keyword and the others of the alphabet must then be laid out as a 5 × 5 grid (with 'y' and 'z' sharing a square):

S	P	L	I	N
T	E	R	A	B
C	D	F	G	H
J	K	M	O	Q
U	V	W	X	Y/Z

In this cipher, unlike the earlier ones, letters are coded not singly but in pairs. To start with, then, you must split up the letters of your message, 'Happy Birthday', to form:

▶ **HA PP YB IR TH DA YQ**

(Conventionally you add a 'q' to any message that has an odd number of letters.) The precise substitution used for each pair depends on the position of the two letters in the grid. Using for our examples this particular grid, the rules are as follows:

▶ If the two letters are in the same row, replace them by the letters immediately to their right. If one of the letters is at the end of its row, imagine that the row is continuous – so that the next letter to the right of the right-hand one is the first letter of the same row. Thus

EA becomes **RB**
DH becomes **FC**

▶ If the two letters are in the same column, replace them by the letters immediately beneath them. If one of the letters is at the bottom of its column, imagine that the column is continuous – so that the next letter beneath the one at the bottom is the letter at the top of the same column. Thus

RM becomes **FW**
AX becomes **GI**

▶ If the letters are in neither of these relative positions, consider them as the diagonally opposite corners of a square or rectangle. The pair of letters is then replaced by those at the other two corners of the square or rectangle. Note the order in which this is done: the lower of the two letters in the grid matches the lower of the other two corner-letters, the upper matches the upper. Thus

RO becomes **AM**
YS becomes **UN**
FT becomes **CR**

▶ If the pair consists of the same letter repeated, like the PP of HA PP YB IR TH DA YQ, the second letter is replaced by an uncommon one, conventionally Q. Thus

read **PP** as **PQ**, which coded becomes **NK**

So, if you were using 'splinter' as your keyword, your 'Happy Birthday' message to your friend would become 'Gbnkn Hlabcgen' – your slow-on-the-uptake friend may believe you've added Martian to the languages you speak! If you're still unclear about the rules for substitution, try working out the 'translation' for yourself:

HA PP YB IR   TH   DA YQ
GB NK NH LA   BC   GE NY

A PARTING WORD!

–	REAT
–	UTER
–	RGAN
–	ANCE
–	INGE
–	OUNG
–	AGER

–	AICH	–
–	NRUS	–
–	DAGI	–
–	UM	–
–	ITTL	–

▶ Person addressed during family outing (3)

▶ My **1**, **5**, **1** is what I spy with
My **4**, **2**, **1** is 1
My **3**, **4**, **1**, **5** is a baby kangaroo
My **7**, **6**, **2** is where Daniel went

1	- - -	–	2	- - - -	–	3	- - - - -
4	- -	–	5	- - -	–	6	- - - -
7	- - -	–	8	- - - -	–	9	- - - - -
10	- - -	–	11	- - - -	–	12	- - - - -

1 Anger
2 *The – – – – of Spring*
3 Pawnee or Cherokee, for example
4 – – *Kill a Mockingbird*
5 *The Long – – – Summer*
6 Given by an owl or someone who cares

7 A short answer
8 Ache
9 Rubinstein's instrument
10 Assam or Oolong, for example
11 Place in Parliament or on train
12 What Sonja Henie used to do – fish?

G	REAT
O	UTER
O	RGAN
D	ANCE
B	INGE
Y	OUNG
E	AGER

T	AICH	**I**
O	NRUS	**H**
A	DAGI	**O**
L	UM	**P**
L	ITTL	**E**

▶ **YOU**

▶ **ENJOYED**

1	IRE	T	**2**	RITE	B	**3**	TRIBE
4	TO	H	**5**	HOT	O	**6**	HOOT
7	NAP	I	**8**	PAIN	O	**9**	PIANO
10	TEA	S	**11**	SEAT	K	**12**	SKATE

BIBLIOGRAPHY

Augarde, Tony: *The Oxford Guide to Word Games*. London and Oxford, Oxford University Press, 1984

Brandreth, Giles: *The World's Best Indoor Games*. New York, Pantheon Books, 1981

Cochrane, James (editor): *The Dictionary Game Dictionary*. Edinburgh, W. & R. Chambers, 1988

Collins Gem Guides: *Family and Party Games*. London, HarperCollins and the Diagram Group, 1990

Collins Gem Guides: *Games for One*. London, HarperCollins and the Diagram Group, 1992.

Collins Gem Guides: *Travel Games*. London, HarperCollins and the Diagram Group, 1992

Eckler, A. Ross: *Word Recreations*. New York, Dover Books, 1972

Espy, William R.: *The Game of Words*. New York, Grosset & Dunlap, 1971

Fisher, John: *The Magic of Lewis Carroll*. London, Thomas Nelson, 1973

Gardner, Martin: *Codes, Ciphers and Secret Writing*. New York, Simon & Schuster, 1972 (available in 1984 Dover Books edition)

Meyer, Jerome: Puzzle, *Quiz and Stunt Fun* (2nd edition). New York, Dover Books, 1972

Wetterau, Bruce (editor): *The Complete Word-Finder Crossword Dictionary*. New York, New American Llbrary, 1981

Wood, Clement, and Goddard, Gloria: *The Complete Book of Games*. New York, Halcyon House, 1940

INDEX